TINY
HOUSES
BUILT WITH
RECYCLED
MATERIALS

TINY HOUSES
BUILT WITH
RECYCLED MATERIALS

Inspiration for Constructing
Tiny Homes Using Salvaged
and Reclaimed Supplies

Ryan Mitchell, author of *Tiny House Living*

Adams Media
New York   London   Toronto   Sydney   New Delhi

DEDICATION

To those who supported me in my dream to live tiny and beyond.

SPECIAL THANKS

A special thanks to Amy Annette Henion.

Aadamsmedia

Adams Media
An Imprint of Simon & Schuster, Inc.
57 Littlefield Street
Avon, Massachusetts 02322

For information about special discounts for bulk purchases, please contact Simon & Schuster Special Sales at 1-866-506-1949 or business@simonandschuster.com.

The Simon & Schuster Speakers Bureau can bring authors to your live event. For more information or to book an event contact the Simon & Schuster Speakers Bureau at 1-866-248-3049 or visit our website at www.simonspeakers.com.

Manufactured in the United States of America

10 9 8 7 6 5 4 3 2

Library of Congress Cataloging-in-Publication Data has been applied for.

ISBN 978-1-4405-9211-9
ISBN 978-1-4405-9212-6(ebook)

Cover photographs by Christian Parsons, Tiny House Expedition; Rocky Mountain Tiny Houses; Alicia Fox Photography; Wendy Barrington; Mark Miller; A. Hall; Hummingbird Micro Homes.

Interior photographs by Aaron Maret; Christian Parsons, Tiny House Expedition; April Anson; Wendy Barrington; A. Hall; Laila Alamiri; Conrad Rogue; Nat Rea Photography; Khari Scott and Dominique Moody; Hummingbird Micro Homes; Rocky Mountain Tiny Houses; Alicia Fox Photography, www.aliciafoxphotography.com; Kate Fox; The Local Branch; Jessica Humiston; Mark Miller; Max Cooper Photography; Tamara Gavin; Sarah G. Hastings; rawrestorations.com; Erin Leigh Pasternak, www.erinpasternak.com; Guillaume Dutilh.

Frame photograph © Leszek Glasner/123RF; Folded paper house photograph © Kanate Chainapong; Graph paper illustration © Kanate Chainapong; Wood plank wall photograph © Weerapat Kiatdumrong; Paperclip illustration © bryljaev.

CONTENTS

Part I: Reclaiming Tiny Houses **7**

Chapter 1: Why Tiny? Why Reclaimed?   9

Chapter 2: Reclaiming Materials   19

Part II: Talking to Tiny House Owners **35**

April Anson   37

Jamie, Wendy, Avery, & Gabe Barrington   43

Stacey's Airstream   49

Makayla Cavanagh   55

Kate Fox & Andy Gill   61

James Galletly   67

Tiny Hall House   71

Sarah Hastings   79

Zee Kesler   83

Aaron Maret   89

Mark Miller 97

Dominique Moody 101

Greg Parham 105

Natalie Pollard 111

Gareth Roberts 115

Conrad Rogue 121

Alexis Stephens & Christian Parsons 127

Cherie Southwick 133

Dan & Jess Sullivan 137

Blaine & Mackenzie Vossler 141

Closing 147

Resources 149

Index 153

About the Author 157

PART I

RECLAIMING

TINY

HOUSES

WHY TINY? WHY RECLAIMED?

Tiny houses have captured the imagination of people for more than a decade now. The promise of affordable housing is an enticing proposition in today's world. We see people struggling to find themselves in this modern age, a time defined by "bigger is better," "keeping up with the Joneses," and a mentality that tells us we must always strive for more, go faster, and achieve perfection.

Tiny houses stand in stark contrast to this outlook. Small homes, which typically range from 100 to 400 square feet, have drawn much attention as a viable alternative to traditional housing because of cost, design sense, and environmental friendliness.

In this book we profile tiny houses of all shapes, sizes, and styles, which embody the spirit of the movement. These homes are built with a purpose: to pare down on space and possessions in order to focus on the important things in life.

While many want tiny houses to be confined in a neat box, the truth is a tiny house, at its core, is about breaking preconceived notions of what a house is.

The essence of a tiny home is not the square footage, it is not space-saving storage, it is not a particular style or design practice. Rather, a tiny house is a structure that provides everything you need to live your best life in the most efficient and cost-effective manner possible.

A tiny house is a home that conforms to the following three principles:

1. It focuses on effective use of space.
2. It relies on good design to meet the needs of the residents.
3. It serves as a vehicle to a lifestyle that the resident wishes to pursue.

A tiny home for a family of four might be 1,000 square feet. For one single person a house of 150 square feet might be right, while another individual might want 300 square feet. All of these are tiny houses.

Reclaimed Materials and Their Role in Tiny Houses

There is often a correlation between people who are interested in tiny homes and people who are both environmentally conscious and budget minded. Their ethos are closely aligned. It is no surprise then that we find a lot of people using reclaimed materials in tiny houses.

Many looking to make the move into a tiny house are looking for a more affordable way to live. Others want to live in a home that is gentle on the earth and lessens their impact. Reclaimed materials are great in meeting both of these goals.

Lots of people don't have enough funds to build a home, so using reclaimed materials is the only way to make the construction of a house possible. They don't want to spend years saving, so using reclaimed materials can cut down on the time to when they can walk in the front door. Time and money are both precious commodities, and using reclaimed materials as a way to achieve your dream of living in a tiny home more quickly can have a profound impact on the trajectory of your life.

There are others who are drawn to the aesthetics of reclaimed materials, the rich tones aged wood can bring, the unique look of their house that comes from materials with a history. Often using salvaged materials can lead to innovations, creating homes with a lot of character. Many people like the fact that they are able to design and build a house that is purpose-built to their lives, their tastes, and their needs.

This is a strong contrast with modern-day tract homes, which are built "on spec" and optimized for an "ideal buyer," a data-driven profile created by market research. That research is used to create a home that appeals to the largest segment of home buyers. What this means is today's modern homebuilding isn't really built *for* anyone; it's built to maximize sale and resale. The person who lives in that home doesn't get a house built for her or his life but for someone else's.

Finally tiny house people love reclaimed materials because they allow for a story. The story comes both from the life that the materials afford them in a tiny house and the stories from the materials themselves. Obtaining reclaimed materials is a complex process. You must interact with many different people to piece together the materials for your house. Such a process, finding everything you need, often requires a strong social network of individuals. Through all our interviews with people who used reclaimed materials in their homes, we found they had to construct a strong web of relationships for their homes to be completed. This brings a narrative of connected humans and objects to each of these houses.

All these things add up to stories about the people who helped you build your tiny home and the materials that ended up in it—stories that you then share with others when they come into the tiny house. In building your home, you are writing the next chapter in that material's story.

Tiny Home Cost

A huge advantage of tiny houses and, in particular, the ones that use reclaimed materials, is their cost. The expense of a tiny house pales in comparison to that of a traditional house. The cost of housing has grown dramatically over the past sixty-five years. This is particularly noticeable today when income has stagnated. In 1950 the median household income was $4,237 and the average house cost was $7,354 for an income to home cost equivalent of 1.7. Compared to today, the median household income is $51,939 and the average house cost is $343,300 for an income to home cost equivalent of 6.6.

This sharp increase means that most people can no longer afford to purchase a home. Even if they are able to earn enough to qualify for a mortgage, more and more homeowners owe more on their mortgage than they can actually earn in a standard working life. Mortgages used to have fifteen-year terms; today the norm is thirty years, but we are beginning to see a rise in forty-year mortgages and reverse mortgages just to make owning a home possible.

Considering the average home in America sold for $341,500 in 2015, tiny houses are a breath of fresh air. The average tiny home built by its owner costs an average of $20,000, a price easily achievable for many people with a few years' savings. The houses we profile in this book range in cost from $7,000 to $25,000, the average being around $13,000.

Tiny Home Design

Beyond the cost of the home, tiny houses are an attractive option because of their design. Often a

great deal of care is devoted to their aesthetics and layout. They are homes that are built and designed from the ground up for the occupant, because to live in such a small space, you must have it perfectly customized to you.

Tiny home designers focus on both the structural and social aspects of a home. How does the design impact how its owner interacts with the space? How do the placement and design choices of storage, seating, windows, and materials impact the feeling of the space? Does the storage hide clutter to promote a clear mind? Do the windows extend the sight line to make the home feel bigger? Do the materials provide a warm sensory experience?

It is this attention to details and interactions that people find so appealing. Modern home designs largely ignore these things, so it is a breath of fresh air to many when they see quality design. Modern cookie-cutter neighborhoods are predicated on designs that maximize profits, not the owner's happiness. Large-scale builders strive to minimize lot sizes to increase the number of units per acre. They focus on formulas for optimal marketability, and they cut corners in building quality to such an extent that code enforcers must step in to keep many builders honest.

Good design itself is difficult to put a number to, but the feeling it creates, a comfort within a space, is undeniable. Mass-market homebuilding can't market design, so it concentrates on telling prospective buyers about the number of rooms, square footage, granite countertops, and walk-in closets. While big house Realtors sell to the largest number of people—which they define as their market—they have honed their house designs to a type; anyone outside of that ideal customer has a difficult time buying, building, or selling a home. Today most homebuilders design homes for large families, with extra rooms for entertaining and accommodating guests. As a result many single millennial home buyers are forced to buy homes with multiple bedrooms that will remain mostly empty.

Reclaimed Materials

The use of reclaimed materials in housing is nothing new, but it's seen a recent rise in popularity as people look for unique ways to decorate and build their space. Reclaimed materials have a long history that is rooted in practicality. Reclaiming materials was and is an efficient way to build and maximize what you already have. At a time when hardware stores weren't on every corner selling inexpensive lumber, you saved on the labor of milling boards.

Way back when, cutting trees into dimensional shapes was difficult and labor intensive. Back in the pioneer days, buildings were constructed by hand hewing logs with which to build and later hand sawing them. It was only later that modern lumber mills began processing lumber with methods that didn't require removing material by hand with an axe or hand saw.

Today's mills are advanced operations that precisely monitor moisture, use lasers to scan for perfect cuts, and employ computer-controlled milling to maximize the boards yield per log. Add to this a global transport system allowing for goods to be moved quickly around the world and we now have lumber that is easily accessible and cheap to buy. We've come a long way, but the appeal of reclaimed materials is still ever-present—however, for different reasons.

What Are Reclaimed Materials?

In today's world we often focus on buying new, but there has been a rise in recycled and repurposed materials in all aspects of our lives. Lumber is no different. At its simplest definition reclaimed wood is lumber that was used for one construction project, but is then salvaged and used in another.

Typically when we speak of reclaimed wood, we are talking about wood that was harvested some time ago and possesses some unique attributes that new wood does not. Often people prefer to leave it in its original form, instead of milling it or chipping it. This doesn't have to be the case, but it is often implicit.

Broadly speaking, we can also consider wood that has been recycled to be reclaimed as well. This is a growing trend in the building-material industry as it looks to maximize its use of materials.

There are two main types of recycling in wood products: industrial wood product waste and recaptured wood materials. With any manufacturing operation you will find some waste from the process; in the case of wood product manufacturing, this includes wood pulp, sawdust, and rejected materials. Recaptured wood products are discarded consumer wood products collected in mass, chipped, and then used to make new products; a good example is retired pallets that are chipped and turned into particle board.

Photograph by Aaron Maret

Then there are items besides lumber, such as fixtures, handles, lights, scrap metal sheeting, used windows and doors, along with a whole host of other materials. These items are often kept in their original form and either used again in the same way or reconfigured into new creative uses.

Why Should You Use Reclaimed Materials?

As is the case with tiny houses, the reasons for wanting to use reclaimed materials are varied. Reclaimed materials offer many opportunities

Photograph by Christian Parsons, Tiny House Expedition

and drawbacks, so it's up to you to determine what makes sense for you to use in your tiny home. Following are some common reasons why people use them.

THEY'RE BUDGET-FRIENDLY MATERIALS

One of the biggest reasons people use reclaimed materials is because they can save a lot of money when it comes to building their home. There are opportunities to reclaim lumber from old buildings, items and fixtures from building salvage stores, and everything and anything from those who no longer need the materials.

You may not have a lot of funds, but you do have free time. In many cases it's enough payment that you can show up and haul away the materials. In this way you're able to gain building materials for free. In many cases you'll have to act quickly so it's important to be flexible and ready to take advantage of opportunities that present themselves.

THEY'RE AN ECOFRIENDLY ALTERNATIVE

The lumber industry is a destructive one—by its very nature it cuts down trees to be fashioned into wood products. We have seen a lot of progress on this front with sustainable harvesting practices, more efficient use of trees, and greater environmental protections put into place, but in the end, lumbering is a damaging practice.

With reclaimed lumber, not only are you offsetting the use of new wood, but you are preventing that used wood from entering a landfill. Upcycling materials and displacing them from waste streams make this an ecofriendly activity.

By not purchasing new wood products we reduce the number of living trees that must be harvested. Currently 900 million trees are cut down each year; this represents a huge impact on our ecosystem. To put this in perspective, the average tree will sequester 1 ton of carbon in a forty-year period. In any given year a mature tree will produce enough oxygen for two human beings.

The damage is not just to the trees themselves but to the earth's capacity to sustain life and maintain homeostasis. At the scale which trees are harvested each year, we begin to see how this can add up to create a long-term impact.

Going to places such as the Habitat for Humanity ReStore, a local salvage yard, or a similar place, capturing fixtures and other building materials before they enter into the waste stream . . . these things can have a big impact. Many of the items you can capture are still in good working order, some of them almost new, and many are available at a good price.

YOU CAN GET QUALITY MATERIALS

The quality of older-growth woods is undeniable. With reclaimed materials that are a few decades older or more, the wood quality is much higher in terms of wood grain, strength, cure, and fiber stability.

Older-growth woods tend to have a much denser fiber structure. This compares favorably to today's lumber. The industry selects trees that grow quickly; this produces larger grains that are less tightly packed. The tighter the wood fibers, the stronger the wood, the more durable it is, and the better it is to work with.

Tighter fibers allow for a better-quality end product because this kind of wood tends to finish well. Woodworking is essentially the removal of material and then joining one piece to another. With a denser pack of fibers, we can better control the cuts and finish the wood in a more refined manner.

Another benefit of reclaimed wood is that it is often very stable. As with all natural materials a certain amount of warping will occur. With older wood, the grains have twisted to their full extent, and this means the wood will generally stay in its shape better than newer boards.

Even if the wood is warped you can either use it as is, highlighting its character, or you can remill it. There still is a chance that it will warp depending on air moisture, but it's usually less than is the case with new wood.

It is worth noting that some people find older woods more difficult to cut because of the fiber density. In some cases it may require higher-powered tools to handle the denser material, particularly in the case of your table saw and router.

When it comes to fixtures and other hard goods, many people like the older styles of the items. Many also appreciate the quality that you

Photograph by Aaron Maret

can find; older things often were made to last longer and be more durable than those we turn out today.

IT'S GOT A UNIQUE CHARACTER

The rise in popularity of reclaimed woods is often attributed to their character or the aesthetic qualities of the wood itself. Aging older wood often contains rich colors, which are hard to replicate through artificial techniques.

In aging, wood tends to take on two major tones, depending on how it was kept. Exposed to the elements, reclaimed wood will take on a shade of gray. These grays will vary depending on the type of wood, climate, and exposure. On the other hand, with prolonged exposure to the sun wood often suffers from UV degradation. This type of wood should only be used in accent pieces, not structural pieces. Wood that is protected from sun and most moisture often cures in brown tones, and because it isn't exposed to UV rays, it often cures harder as the resins in the board dry and solidify.

You will often find unique patterns in reclaimed wood; these derive from how the pieces were processed. You'll find old nail holes, saw blade patterns, or a chipped look that comes from the wood being hand hewn. These unique looks add character to your tiny house and tell the story of the wood.

IT HAS UNIQUE DIMENSIONS

Today's lumber is uniform: You have two-by-fours, four-by-fours, and so on. In older times, lumber often lacked uniformity in the dimensions of the wood because they were often determined by the size of the tree or resulted from the lack of precision of hand tools. Older-growth trees were generally larger. They yielded a wider board and longer beams.

Much of today's lumber is often only available in smaller widths. Larger sizes cost a lot more—if you can even find them at all. The main reason for this is that most of today's harvested trees are between twelve and twenty-four inches in diameter, compared to older lumber that was often milled from much larger trees. By comparison older-growth trees can be much bigger depending on the species; old-growth poplar trees can be six feet, an oak tree can be nine feet, and a redwood tree can grow to twenty-seven feet or more in diameter.

IT COMES WITH STORIES

One thing that has struck me while talking to people who use reclaimed materials in their tiny houses is the stories that they tell about their reclaimed items. I think these stories are an interesting and often overlooked benefit of reclaimed materials.

Often the stories are about a key piece of the home, an accent feature, or focal point. When out and about collecting the materials, scrounging them from different places, you meet interesting people who tell you about themselves. The materials too have a history, a place that they came from, a life before they were part of your home.

The story could be an interesting or bizarre encounter with the previous owner, the struggle to get that material, or a past use that makes it interesting. Regardless, using reclaimed materials builds that history, adding a new chapter as the materials are gathered, worked, and reborn.

Benefits and Negatives of Using Reclaimed Materials

Pros	Cons
Can be less expensive	Can be more time intensive
Visual character and uniqueness	Nonstandard sizes of wood
Denser grain, higher quality	Requires more labor to prepare for use
Materials with a story	More difficult to source materials
Inspires unique designs	Harder to plan; materials drive design
Environmentally friendly	Inefficiencies from sourcing uses more fossil fuels
Wood more stable, less likely to warp	Pests and mold may come with wood
Can be more durable from tighter grain	Unknown previous treatments (lead paint, chemicals, etc.)
Minimizes forest destruction	May require additional tools for processing

Building for the Future

As we move into the future, reclaimed and recycled materials are going to need to become a larger part of building structures for ourselves. We currently use recycled materials in some of our engineered wood products, but moving forward we need to increase our ability to capture more recyclable waste and find uses for it in our structures; doing so will bring our use of wood into a more sustainable future.

We are quickly approaching a point when we must grapple with the reality that harvesting wood the way we do today is not sustainable in the long term. Even with planned forestry, selective cutting, and efficiencies in our manufacturing processes we can't displace the destructive nature of the practice.

For a variety of reasons it is difficult for us to make decisions as a global community. Our world operates on an economy that is predicated on perpetual growth on a planet with finite resources. Impacts are externalized to places we do not see and motivated by the drive for immediate profits.

It is difficult to steer a new course when there is so much wealth being accumulated by those who have a vested interest in seeing the status quo maintained. That said, the tides are turning.

We need to turn our focus to harvesting from existing wood sources; we must draw materials from buildings that need to be dismantled or demolished. This is, of course, already happening but on a very small scale, one that is not making a dent in the market. What we need is larger-scale operations that harvest wood from unused buildings en masse. It is at this scale, one where we could supply chipped wood in the hundreds of thousands of tons a year, that we can begin to move from live forest harvesting to reclaimed harvesting.

With sources such as these we can then design building materials to use chipped reclaimed wood. We can shape it into wood stud equivalents, into dimensional lumber replacements, and into other wood-based products that we use every day. The technology will be developed to match these, including more sustainable and environmentally friendly resins to bind these chipped materials together. However, without the source material (large-scale reclaimed chipped wood) there is no drive to expend R & D dollars on these innovations.

RECLAIMING MATERIALS

Unlike buying new materials, there are two major considerations when it comes to using reclaimed materials: sourcing and processing. While some places are fortunate enough to have resources that reclaim materials and then sell them in one spot, many people find their only option is to scour their social networks and online sources.

Even once you locate the materials, some work is often required to get them into a useable state. They may not be in a uniform dimension, the wood may have metal fasteners in it, there may be layers of paint that must be scraped off, and so on.

The challenge with reclaimed materials is that even when you do find a good source of materials, you often cannot find uniform pieces, the quantities are small, and they require some work to get them ready.

Estimating Required Materials

Finding sources may be the biggest challenge when it comes to using reclaimed materials; however

there are some good go-to places to look. First, though, we must determine what we are looking for.

Spend some time deciding what types of parameters you are going to look for in the materials that you encounter. Ask yourself these questions:

1. What will the materials be used for in your tiny house?
2. Will the materials be used for a structural piece, an aesthetic trim piece, or do you need both?
3. What types of wood will you need: sheet goods, dimensional lumber, larger beams, etc.?
4. How many pieces will you need in board feet?
5. What is the longest span of wood in your design that you'll need to gather?
6. What are some things that would cause you to decline to take certain lumber?

It is important to understand how the reclaimed elements that you have gathered will find their way into your design. It can be tricky to make actual plans for your house when a lot of the materials will vary widely. You may well find you have to adjust your plans.

There are, however, some elements common to all homes, from which we can generate some rough numbers to use as goals in our search for reclaimed materials. I suggest that if you're going to be framing with reclaimed wood, you do some of these calculations ahead of time so you know how much material you'll need to collect. This will make the building process go much more smoothly.

Sample Wall Estimation

Estimated Wood Needs for Walls			
PART	NUMBER	MEASUREMENTS	NOTES
Studs	35	8' 2 × 4s	46' of wall at 16" on center
Wall plates	10	8' 2 × 4s	Two 8'-wide & two 20'-wide walls
Double top plate	8	8' 2 × 4s	To join pieces of walls
Window #1	3	8' 2 × 4s	Framing for window box
Window #2	3	8' 2 × 4s	Framing for window box
Window #3	3	8' 2 × 4s	Framing for window box
Window #4	3	8' 2 × 4s	Framing for window box
Door	4	8' 2 × 4s	Framing for door frame
L wheel well	3	8' 2 × 4s	Framing to box in left trailer wheel well
R wheel well	3	8' 2 × 4s	Framing to box in right trailer wheel well
Internal wall	9	8' 2 × 4s	Internal wall frame for bathroom
Subtotal	84	8' 2 × 4s	Rounded up
Extra 15%	13	8' 2 × 4s	Extra for mistakes and unusable leftovers
Total	**97**	**8' 2 × 4s**	**Rounded up**

All tiny houses have framing; these are typically made up of a 2 × 4 (which is actually 1½" × 3½") studs that are spaced 16" on center. Windows and doors are typically framed with headers, "cripple" plates, and sills. Finally, roof framing is built with a ridge beam and rafters.

For walls take your total length of all your walls and assume an 8' stud every 16" of that wall. Doing this basic math, you can then estimate the number of studs you'll need to gather. For example if you have 46' of walls with studs every 16", you know you'll need 35 boards that are around 8' long and roughly the size of a 2 × 4.

A typical wall, built by framing lumber, consists in its simplest form of three main parts: a top plate, wall studs, and a bottom plate. The bottom plate is most often a 2 × 4 that lies on the floor of your house. Vertical studs then attach to the bottom plate, perpendicular to it. Finally the top plate is attached on top of the studs, going in the same direction as the bottom plate. These three parts are nailed together to form the structure of a wall. Things become more complicated and require more materials as you add things like windows and doors, but the same form persists.

You can then assume that you'll need a top and bottom plate the length of the walls. If it's a 20'-wide wall, we know that realistically we aren't going to find such a long piece. If you're unable to find a board that spans the entire distance of the wall then you'll need to create the wall out of 8' wall sections; then add a layer on top of the top plates (double top plate with offset seams) to join the 8' sections together.

This will add to the number of boards you will need, but it allows you to use short pieces where you can offset the seams of shorter boards to create a longer-spanning plate. In the previous example we estimated we'd need 6 boards for the top plate and the bottom plates of the wall framings (done in 8' sections), then another 3 boards to join all the walls together by creating a double top plate to tie it all together.

Finally we estimated the number of windows, doors, and internal walls in the tiny house to give us our final required 2 × 4s estimated number of 84. We then assumed an additional 15 percent more boards will be needed because of mistakes or not being able to fully use the wood scraps in the framing. If you're a first-time builder, it might be smart to raise this to 25 percent just in case. You can always find other uses for the wood you don't use.

With this example you can begin to see how to create a list of required materials, which forms a "shopping list" of items you need to find when you source your materials. You can conduct similar estimates with your build. Estimate:

- Roof framing
- Floor framing
- Sheathing
- Siding
- Roofing
- Windows
- Flooring
- Interior trim work

From this process—which is time consuming, but valuable—you create a master shopping list that allows you to more accurately estimate what you need to have on hand for your build. Having a list such as this means you know when you're ready to build, gives you an idea of how things will all fit together, and allows you to build faster.

Sourcing Materials

Finding materials is usually one of the more challenging parts of using reclaimed wood. While some cities have great sources for reclaimed materials, others don't offer much. In general sources of reclaimed wood fall into three main categories: commercial operations, online listings, and personal networking.

In many cities around the country we are beginning to see businesses opening smaller-scale reclaiming operations that source, process, and sell wood (and often other reclaimed materials) to customers. These commercial operations often work closely with the building community to take advantage of materials that would otherwise be thrown away.

Probably the best-known operation is the Habitat for Humanity ReStore, which takes old building materials they either received via donations or took out of houses they reclaimed. There are other smaller shops that do similar things all around the nation, providing great places to source materials.

The next major source for materials is online listings; many websites connect people who are trying to get rid of stuff (for sale or for free) with those looking for various items. The two most popular online connecting points mentioned in interviews for this book were Craigslist.org and Freecycle.org.

Craigslist offers two main categories you can explore for reclaimed materials: Free and For Sale. While the For Sale section implies a cost, you can often barter for the items or find great deals.

One of our interviewees, Zee Kesler, told us about a strategy she often uses when finding things for sale online. She contacts the sellers and asks if they'll consider letting her have the items for free if she loads them up and takes them away that same day. Many times, she says, people decline, but Zee then counters and says, "The offer still stands; I'll check back in a week." She waits a week, and in many cases the items have not been sold and the person has reached a point where she or he just wants the thing gone. In the end she has been able to get many things for free.

In the Free section of Craigslist you have to be very quick to move in on free materials. It is often a first-come-first-served arrangement. One tip we learned from our interviews is that you can set up a keyword search on your phone, using Craigslist's RSS feeds to alert you every time a new posting containing the keywords goes live.

There's an App for That

Apps such as Feeddler allow you to tie into their RSS feed and input certain keywords for notifications. Some keywords you might consider:

- Wood
- Barn wood
- Lumber
- Scrap wood
- Pallets

It might also be worthwhile to try alternate spellings, hyphenations, common misspellings, and colloquial terms. These search parameters are important because the apps look for the exact matches to what you input. So, for example, if you enter "barn wood" and someone listed it under "barnwood" or "barn-wood" or "wood from barn" you would not see these in your search results unless you included all of them as search parameters in the app.

Setting up this type of system on your smartphone will instantly alert you to new stuff that may be worth checking out, and being first to know gives you an edge. Combine this with a flexible schedule and a handy way to pick up and transport the materials, and you can discover some great stuff.

Freecycle is a service designed to connect people who have things that they don't want to people who are looking for those items, often for free. The website emphasizes environmental motivations, to keep things out of landfills.

Just as with Craigslist, it's important to check Freecycle often because things tend to move quickly, particularly the really good items. Some communities have websites set up for their local Freecycle, while others have mailing lists that you join. In some cases you can set up RSS notifications for this as well.

Networking

The final source for reclaimed materials is from your own social network. This can be both online and offline, but it relies on your personal relationships. The best way to start is by doing the initial legwork to understand what you will need to build your tiny house.

From there consider how you can pick up, transport, and store the items. During my build of my own tiny house, I had a very small car, so I decided to install a trailer hitch on my car and was able to find a free trailer on which I could load materials so I could transport them home. This made the task easy and kept my car clean.

Once you have a good idea of what you need and how you can transport it, start reaching out. Many tiny house builders have found it useful to make a simple poster, which they hand out to friends and family, and post throughout their local community. On this they explain why they need the materials to build a tiny house, what they are looking for, and how to get in contact with them.

When considering who to reach out to, it's best to throw a wide net. You never know who might be a good source; materials often come from unlikely sources. Don't just ask people if they have materials—find out if they know someone who has materials or would be a good lead.

Exploring each connection and referral is a time-consuming venture, but the connections that you build can lead to new friends. They can also lead to a great source for materials or some other positive outcome. The truth is you don't really know where it will all lead, but it's an important part of using reclaimed materials.

Talk It Out

When talking to people who do have materials make sure that you understand what it is they are offering, what they want in return (if anything), and how you can make it easy for them to give you materials. Some people will be really excited about your tiny house because they think it's interesting. Others don't care much what you're going to do with the materials; they just want you to take them away. Time and time again I've seen situations where people just want to clear out their wood shop. All they really care about is if you're going to take it all and load it yourself. They may or may not be interested in tiny houses, but what they really care about is how you're going to help them solve the problem of having too much stuff.

Do your best to anticipate their concerns and their objections, and find ways to make their lives a little bit easier when it comes to giving you these things. Offer to take all the materials; be sure to communicate that you will load the materials yourself; be flexible to best suit their schedule. Do these things, and you'll find a lot of people willing to help you out with free materials.

At the same time, know when to say "no." There will be times that you arrive and discover that the materials are not as they were described. It may not be what you need, the wood may be rotted, or it isn't useable (too small, to short, not structurally sound). It can be tricky to say no to someone, particularly when you've shown up at her house to rifle through her woodpile, but you need to navigate that social situation with honesty and courtesy.

One of the biggest lessons that we learned from talking to the tiny home builders who used reclaimed materials was that in the beginning they didn't know how to say no. This meant they got a lot of materials they couldn't use, and then they were stuck with them. In many cases stuff piled up during the build and the homeowners ended up paying to have it disposed of. Many people in our interviews said that saying no to materials they couldn't use was a big shift for them, but it was a necessary one.

Evaluating Materials

Once you find sources for your materials you need to evaluate them to determine if they suit your needs. This can be a difficult thing. When evaluating materials it is important to know if the item will be a structural piece, meaning it needs to carry a load, or an aesthetic piece, for looks only and not load bearing.

Load-bearing or structural pieces of lumber are essential to the integrity of your tiny home. Many people argue that structural pieces should always be new in order to minimize risks associated with reclaimed woods. It's true that using reclaimed wood for structural pieces is a risk, one that you'll need to evaluate. Consider the repercussions or liability if something bad happens.

While older lumber typically has a tighter grain and thus is stronger and more durable, this fact doesn't mean reclaimed wood is always the proper choice for load-bearing purposes. When considering a piece, look at how it was stored and where it existed when it was in use. You want pieces that were protected from the elements, particularly ones that were shaded from the sun and kept away from moisture.

When it comes to integrity, sun and moisture are wood's two biggest enemies. Prolonged sun exposure can cause UV damage. The UV rays degrade the wood to the point that it can become brittle. They can also reduce its strength

considerably. Water can soak into wood and begin to break it down with mold and rot.

Damage caused by bugs and pests can also be a cause for concern. Termites, ants, and other insects can bore into the wood and hollow it out from the inside. Making sure that the wood isn't damaged or even worse, still infested with bugs can be difficult to determine, but this is important to know before you start using the wood in your build.

Examine the materials for previous fastener infiltration. As with any wood, reclaimed or new, every time you put in a fastener or drill a hole, you weaken the integrity of the wood. With enough holes or points of infiltration, the wood can weaken so that it can be easily broken with enough force. Consider the previous fastener holes and how you plan to use them rather than making new ones.

If there are already holes near the place where you'll need to create new ones, it might make sense to use a different piece of wood. A good rule of thumb is that a nail or screw should have a 1"-diameter circle of clear, undamaged wood around it.

When you fasten the board in its new position, make the hole cleanly with the fastener; make sure that no cracks or other structural defects form around the fastener.

When in doubt, find another option for structural pieces, even if it means going to a new piece. Paying a little extra for a higher-quality reclaimed material or choosing a new option can go a long way in ensuring your safety and peace of mind. In the end, you assume all responsibility for your choices.

Processing Materials

Once you locate and transport your materials back to your build site, there are several things to consider about processing the wood. This is the time- and labor-intensive part of using reclaimed materials, but establishing a system, having the right tools on hand, and doing a little planning can make the process much easier.

Processing the materials as they come in allows you to work more efficiently, store more compactly, and spread the workload evenly. From the interviews we learned that the task of processing the materials took a lot of time and effort. The following tips will help streamline that workload.

Key Tools

Luckily when it comes to using reclaimed materials you don't need to purchase or borrow a lot of specialized tools above and beyond what you'd need anyway to build a tiny house.

The first main category of tools is nail-removal devices: mainly a claw hammer, a pry bar, and a pair of vice grip pliers. Whenever you reclaim materials, it is a safe bet that there will be nails and screws to remove from the wood. Having these standard tools is both useful and inexpensive.

Another tool for this task is a pallet pry bar. This is a long-handled hook designed specifically for breaking apart pallets; it hooks under the slat of a pallet, and its fulcrum rests on the main skid allowing for you to more easily remove the slat.

The next category of reclaiming tools is those used for resurfacing. When working with reclaimed materials it is often necessary to clean up and square the edges and surfaces of the wood. The go-to tools for this are a sander (orbital and belt), table saw, and surface planer.

While many tiny house people don't want to spring for a planer, most of the people we spoke with who built their tiny houses with reclaimed materials used one extensively. The other tools, table saw and sander, are needed in order to build a tiny house and are very useful in getting materials to a useable state for the build.

Re-sawing and milling are other parts of the process for which you need specialized tools. Builders use them for milling wood from a full tree into dimensional lumber and re-sawing larger pieces of dimensional lumber into smaller pieces. In many cases people don't do much if any of this because it's a bit more involved than they want.

For those of you who want to do this, though, you can use portable band saw mills for milling raw trees into lumber. These can process large logs into boards and beams. In many cases you can find mobile band saw mills that will come to your property and for a per-hour rate, mill lumber from felled trees. These portable mills are commonly found in the For Hire sections of Craigslist.

Some people use a special jig for a chainsaw to mill wood, but this tends to produce a less-clean cut than that of the band saw mills; on the other hand, the chainsaw mill option is much cheaper (a few hundred dollars versus several thousand). When milling your own lumber, after cutting it to a rough dimension, you then need to let the wood cure. Air-drying green wood takes one to two years. Alternately you can dry the wood with the aid of a kiln, which typically takes one to two days, depending on the type of wood. The latter heats the wood to a certain temperature and more quickly dries the boards. Once the green wood has been dried, you can mill it into its final size.

For re-sawing, you are taking larger pieces of dried dimensional lumber and cutting them into smaller pieces. For this a shop band saw is most often the best option; however you can also do it with a table saw.

The final main category of tools is safety equipment. While most of this is the same for any woodworking or building project, one piece of equipment is unique to reclaiming materials: a metal detector wand.

When starting on any construction project, you should have hearing protection, eye protection, and protection for your hands in the form of gloves or push sticks for your table saws. The metal detector wand is useful for finding nails that you might have missed in your processing. Hidden nails can lead to an injury when you're cutting or fastening later on.

Deconstruction

In some cases you'll be able to find materials that are already in a useable state; they are scraps or they have already been broken down or been taken apart. In other cases you need to break down the materials from their former state. This is often the case when you get the materials from a home that is being demolished.

It is important in the deconstruction and demolition phase to consider your safety. Deconstructing a structure isn't for a layman. There is a recommended process to safely dismantle a building. Even professionals with years of experience know danger still exists. When you're breaking down smaller, more manageable objects, safety concerns still exist and you should take precautions.

A hardhat for larger structures is a good idea to prevent falling debris from hitting you in the head. Thick work gloves are strongly recommended because nails and screws in the wood are a major safety concern. As with any woodworking activity, you should always wear eye protection. Finally, deconstruction is dirty business and often that

means a lot of dust. Wear a respirator to keep air particulates from entering your lungs.

Start by identifying the pieces that meet your needs and pass your criteria. In some cases you may need to remove other parts to gain access to them. For example, you may have to strip down drywall to access the studs. Consider what is attached to the piece you want and what removing it could do to the structural integrity of the pieces around it.

Once you've identified and considered your desired piece, begin removing it by prying or cutting it out. In order to keep the item useable, consider how much damage will occur during the removal process. In some instances you'll be able to cut just below the top of the stud and just above the bottom with a Sawzall. This will gain a 7' board from a normal 8' stud. If that's all you want for your construction, two quick cuts are all you need.

Longer boards are more difficult to reclaim because there are fewer of them. Those that do exist often have more points of attachment to other pieces, so you'll need to consider if it is even possible to remove a useable piece from the structure.

De-Nailing

Once you have the pieces of lumber, an important part of processing the material is de-nailing. Removing the nails makes working with the material easier and safer. By removing nails and screws you can stack the wood more efficiently so it takes up a lot less space.

Removing the nails and screws prevents accidental injuries from sharp metal pieces in the wood, which might cause concern about tetanus. It also makes the wood safe to process with power tools. If a nail is hidden in a board and is run through a saw, it could kick back against the blade and injure you or cause your hand to slip and fall into the path of the blade.

Similarly, when using nail guns if you don't see an existing nail in the wood, the new nail could strike the old fastener and ricochet. When this happens, the nail often curves back toward the user's hand and impales it.

Unfortunately there is no simple way to remove nails besides brute strength. Hammers, pry bars, and vice grip pliers are the common go-to tools to remove nails. When you pair them with some elbow grease, it can be quite effective. If you are unable to draw out nails and screws with the claw of a hammer or pry bar, consider cutting off that part of the wood that contains the nails. This may be possible if it is at the very end and you don't need the full length of the board.

As mentioned earlier, a metal detector is helpful in making sure you don't miss any metal parts in the wood you are processing. While some see this as overkill, it saves you from the dangers of unexpected metal in the wood.

Resurfacing

Once you have removed the metal parts from the wood, it's smart to resurface the wood, especially if other people are going to see it. Things such as studs and interior wall pieces don't need to look aesthetically pleasing, but those parts that will be seen by others will benefit from being cleaned up.

The main question here is whether you want to preserve the aesthetic of the old, rough, and dirty look of the wood. There are times when resurfacing can take that look away, so consider how you will use that piece.

Resurfacing removes a minimal amount of the material from the surfaces. You can do this in a number of ways, but the goal here is to bring about a clean edge and square the wood. When you first get the wood, it will probably have some warp to it, as do all natural materials. Some pieces are so warped that you may find they are unusable or need to be cut down into a smaller straight piece.

In an ideal situation you'd have a tool called a jointer, which allows you to process wood into perfectly square edges to allow accurate cuts and jointing. The problem is that jointers are large machines that are not within the budget of most amateur woodworkers.

You can achieve a similar result with a table-mounted router with a modified gate. There is a plethora of tutorials online about how to do this, but realize that while it does a decent job, it will never be as accurate as a jointer. Once you have achieved two perfectly square sides you can then move to a table saw that has been calibrated to make your cuts.

You can also remove small amounts of material to even out a rough or uneven surface. In some cases you'll need to mill down a board to a desired thickness. To do this you can re-saw a board with a band saw if you need to remove large portions of the material. If you only need to remove a little bit, a surface planer will allow you to clean up a wide board quickly.

It is important to note that a surface planer does not make pieces of wood flat; only jointers do that. It is a common misconception, but the rollers in the planer are very strong and actually force boards that are slightly warped into a flat position before they move the board into the path of the blades, and as the board exits the planer, the board resumes its original shape, leaving it warped.

Many of the people whom we interviewed for this book found a planer to be essential to their use of reclaimed materials. A new planer is an expensive tool; quality models start at around $500, but there's no good substitute for its function, and there's a lot of demand for it. If you're able to find a used planer, we recommend changing out the blades with a new set to ensure you're making clean and true cuts.

Finally if you only need to clean up small portions of smaller pieces, use a sander to take a rougher piece into a presentable state. There are two main types of sanders that we recommend for tiny house builders: a random orbital sander and a belt sander.

Random orbital sanders move in an inconsistent circular motion, which allows the sander to avoid making obvious patterns as you remove the material. Belt sanders have the advantage of removing a lot more material quickly but can create a pattern in the wood because they move in only one direction.

If you use a belt sander, finish with a random orbital sander, starting with a high-grit paper, then moving to finer-grit paper. The only downside to sanders is that they make it hard to produce a truly flat surface over a wide board because you may remove more material in one part of the wood than another. The variations may not be perceivable and if that is the case and you don't join that surface to another it will be fine. You'll run into an issue when you have to join two surfaces together; if those surfaces aren't perfectly flat, you'll be able to see gaps and the joint may not be as strong.

Creating Uniformity

When working with reclaimed materials the variations in sizes of wood can present some unique challenges. In some cases the uneven edges or variations in the material can create a visual effect that is desirable—a way to bring an organic feel to the construction or to add an element of whimsy. In other cases it is important to have crisp edges for joints, to ensure proper coverage or bonding at key structural points.

When you create uniformity in your materials you often bring efficiencies into the equation. When the boards are all the same width, depth, and length you can more quickly use them in the build. This is particularly true whenever you are creating pieces in repetition (siding, flooring, etc.).

When you frame your wall, all the wood must be the same size. If it already is, you can batch out the cuts quickly. When you plane your floorboards to the same thickness, you can quickly lay out and install them. If you decide to side your house with pallet wood, planing and jointing the boards to a common size will make the installation of the entire outside much easier.

Whenever you need uniformity in your materials you inherently bring in efficiencies and in some cases, bring strength to the structure.

Photograph by Aaron Maret

Determining the uniform size of the material can be approached in one of two ways: determine what the ideal end size will be or take into consideration the most common dimension of the material you are reclaiming. If for example you are framing, it's best to use a 2 × 4 stud, and you would be smart to find lumber that size or larger and re-saw it to the appropriate measurement.

Compare this to siding, which doesn't have to be a specific thickness as long as it's uniform. If you notice that most of the wood you are sourcing is a ½" thick or thicker, it makes sense to plane all the wood to a ½" thick. Think about the function and requirements of that material in the context of the whole house.

When you are processing wood to a uniform state do your best to prevent human error. Use jigs to set your cuts, cut all the boards in one direction at the same time, and use guides such as a table saw fence to ensure your cuts are continuously accurate across all the boards.

When using a planer, note that while the unit often has thickness demarcations, those are only so accurate. Ideally you'll set the planer to one setting, then run all the boards through at the same time. If you need to plane even thinner, reset the planer to a thinner setting, and run all the boards through again at one time. This allows you to maintain a uniform cut across all the boards. Keep doing this until you have achieved your desired thickness. Remove waste material put out by the planer as you go because if it builds up inside the planer you run the risk of it clogging and no longer making uniform cuts.

Similarly with jigs, guides, and your table saw fence, set them once and process everything at the same time. This will ensure that your cuts based off that guide will stay consistent.

Storage

The number one thing we heard from all the people we talked to for this book was the importance of storage. Many of them recommended a large space with built-in racks to keep pieces out of the elements. The toughest part of using reclaimed materials is often finding them, and this usually means collecting all of them takes an extended length of time.

If you don't have a place to store materials, the items you find in the beginning may be damaged, rotted, or unusable by the time you find your last pieces. From my experience storage needs to be in a structure of some sort; tarps don't provide enough protection beyond a few days of mild weather.

Longer-term storage should be in a garage, shed, or enclosed trailer, which will keep the wood out of the elements, particularly the rain. Many people noted in their interviews that they wish they had spent some time initially building racks to better sort and access the wood.

When it comes to sorting wood, two approaches were popular. About half the people found sorting the wood by similar length was helpful because when they needed a board of a certain size, they generally knew where to look. Others preferred to stack their wood in the order in which they were going to use it. This allowed them to work from a single pile; more often than not, the top piece was what they needed.

Regardless of your approach, one thing is clear: Having a large storage space is key, and unlike the house you're trying to build, bigger is generally better because it makes accessing easier and the entire process more efficient.

Common Types of Source Materials

Reclaimed materials often come from a few sources: pallets, flooring, and barn wood. Each of these comes with its own set of considerations and challenges.

Pallets

Wood from pallets is an extremely popular source of reclaimed wood. The shipping industry moves millions of pallets a year, and in many cases the receiver finds himself with a lot of left-over pallets that he would rather not pay to dispose of. This is an ideal situation for people who want to use reclaimed materials.

The best place to find pallets is at places that do a lot of shipping and receiving. Warehouses, shipping ports, manufacturers, distributors, and retail stores all use pallets in large quantities. Finding them can be as simple as driving through industrial or commercial sections of town. More often than not, you'll be able to find warehouses and other places with pallets stacked up by a dumpster near the back door.

It is important to get permission from the owner before you take the pallets. While it's usually a safe bet that pallets stacked near a dumpster aren't wanted any more, technically speaking they are still the property of the owner. Even taking things from the dumpster is a legal gray area, and people have been prosecuted for dumpster diving items.

When using pallets you'll find that the wood you reclaim from them generally is of low quality, not something that you really want to rely on for your structural components. However, it can be used for aesthetic pieces.

One major word of warning: Pallets are often treated for bugs and biological contaminants with a variety of processes. The two most popular methods are heat and chemicals. Heat treatments bring the material up to a certain temperature that would kill most bugs. The use of chemicals to kill bugs is a common practice but raises concerns about off-gassing. If you use chemical-treated boards from pallets on the interior of your house, the off-gassing of those boards may result in health problems.

There are many opinions about how to tell heat-treated from chemical-treated wood, but in the end, after speaking to many people with real-world knowledge, I've concluded that there is no reliable method to determine how pallets were treated. I recommend instead to only use reclaimed pallet wood for outdoor applications or in limited indoor applications after an initial off-gassing period of at least six months. Even with these considerations there may still be some risk.

When it comes to breaking down the pallets there seems to be two main schools of thought. The first says to use a pallet pry bar to pull the slats off the main frame. These pry bars are widely available online and make it much easier to break down pallets; numerous people have reported that they are worth the investment.

The second way people separate the slats from the main frame is by cutting. Some people use a reciprocating saw to cut through the nails while others use a circular saw to cut just inside the row of nails. This yields small boards, which are better suited for small woodworking projects or crafts.

In some cases people have gone so far as to use a pry bar to remove the slats, then run them through a planer to create uniform boards. This is particularly popular with tiny house construction to create siding and accent walls.

Rather than breaking the pallets down into boards, some people prefer to use the whole structure as it is. In some cases, builders use the pallets to create the wall structure. While this technique is not recommended, if you do consider this, you should use the pallets in conjunction with other main structural beams to ensure wall integrity. Of the people to whom we talked who used this method, most said they would not do it again; all of them indicated that the pallets were different thicknesses that created a difficult wall to work with. Many were concerned about the strength of the walls.

Flooring

The reclaiming and reuse of flooring is an obvious choice. Hardwood floors typically are made from high-quality lumber that has a clearer grain, is more durable, and generally can be easily reused. Add to this that the worn look of an old floor can bring a lot of character to a house. Using smaller pieces where the old nails at the ends have been cut off means flooring makes a lot of sense to reclaim.

Luckily, reclaimed flooring is a well-recognized commodity in the building industry. There are many commercial operations that specialize in reclaimed floors, making your job of finding it easy. The scraps and leftovers from larger flooring jobs are often enough to floor an entire tiny house, but they wouldn't be useful in most other applications. This means you can often get the floor scraps for free or cheap, sometimes even brand new.

In older buildings the floors were often made from boards that are thicker than modern flooring. You can reclaim the old flooring, plane it down so it looks clean, reinstall it, and refinish it into a good-looking floor.

If you don't source from commercial reclamation operations you'll be able to find options on Craigslist, Freecycle, and by searching for "old building renovations" online. Because flooring is typically installed over subflooring, it isn't a structural piece, so you can focus on the aesthetic qualities, unlike other pieces that need to support major loads like studs or beams.

Barn Wood

There is something special about the wood you find in old barns. It is both beautiful and often of high quality. You will find larger pieces of lumber that were used to build the barn. This makes old barns a unique source of lumber because you can find longer pieces or find larger logs that you can saw into smaller pieces.

A lot of the quality of old barns comes from their age. Barns typically come from an era when older-growth forests were harvested for wood. This means you'll find much larger logs with tighter grains in more exotic or costly species of woods. The patina of these woods is usually very rich, ranging from a deep shade of brown to the bright gray of exposed wood that has weathered years in the elements.

Barn wood that has been exposed to direct sun and rain often is best suited for aesthetic pieces that don't carry much load; their color is often a gray weather look. As a rule of thumb, reclaimed wood that is colored in brown tones often has been shielded from the elements by a roof or was an interior member that was allowed to age and cure; lumber that has been allowed to cure like this often maintains its structural integrity and such a piece may be more suitable for structural parts.

The sourcing of barn wood and the quality of materials you get from both an aesthetic and structural viewpoint make it a good option for any recycled wood project. Several commercial operations exist, and barn wood can also be found through places such as Craigslist. When considering where to find wood, looking at old barns is a great place to start.

PART II

TALKING TO TINY HOUSE OWNERS

THE FOLLOWING SECTION CONTAINS THE STORIES OF TWENTY PEOPLE WHO HAVE BUILT THEIR OWN TINY HOUSES. EACH OF THESE HOUSES FEATURE RECLAIMED MATERIALS, SALVAGED ITEMS, AND OBJECTS THAT WERE RECYCLED, REPURPOSED, OR REUSED IN SOME MANNER.

APRIL ANSON

TINY HOUSE ON WHEELS

- EASTERN OREGON
- 128 SQUARE FEET
- COMPLETED IN 2012

SINK

BATHROOM

STOVE →

CLOSET

PANTRY

SLEEPING LOFT

BOOKSHELVES

BENCH & STORAGE →

OPEN TO MAIN LEVEL

PORCH   DESK

GUEST SLEEPING LOFT

MAIN LEVEL

LOFT LEVEL

"Building a tiny house forced me to take steps to live in it."

Utilities

Electricity: Grid, but wired for solar

Heating/Cooling: Electric

Water: Grid

Water Heating: Tankless water heater

Stove: Propane

Refrigeration: Standard

Toilet: RV/blackwater

Internet: Shared

APRIL ANSON, A PHD
STUDENT IN OREGON, learned
about tiny houses at an environmental conference she attended in 2012. A
master's student at the time, looking
toward six years of doctoral work, she
knew instantly she wanted a small home
of her own. A few short months later
April moved into her tiny house, which
allowed her to "act on environmental
ethics in a more everyday way."

Living in a tiny house was an adjustment
for April. As she describes it, "If I want
to get into shape, I'll sign up for a race
that forces me to train for it. In a tiny
house, building a tiny house, forced me
to take steps to live in it." Even today
April finds that living small, while giving
her a great place to live that allows her to
exist on a student's budget, does have its
downsides.

Photograph by April Anson

Living in a small home has "shaped ways of living in ways I can't tell yet because I'm still in my tiny house," April explains. "There are things that have been trained into me by living tiny." Instead of hosting others, she meets others outside of her home or goes to their houses instead. Rather than hosting dinner parties with friends and family, she more often goes out for dinner.

In the end her home was built of two-thirds reclaimed materials. She spent between six and eight hours a week during the build in what she called "a treasure hunt every day." April learned that you cannot get attached to doing things in a certain way; the materials shaped how things came out.

Photograph by April Anson

Photographs by April Anson

Her build included a lot of reclaimed materials, and not only because she needed to stay on budget. April loves the parts of her home that have stories. She sourced a lot of her materials from the local rebuilding center and ReStore, where she found her sheathing, light fixtures, and other parts of her house.

She chose to keep most of the wood natural and avoided paints. She likes the natural aesthetic of the raw materials, going so far as using smooth stones for handles. April treated the interior of the house by rubbing linseed oil on the wooden surfaces. Her outside shingles are cedar, and the floors were treated with a natural epoxy alternative to give them more durability. While she likes that the fact that these treatments are less toxic than others, April admits that you do need to reapply them once a year to maintain the coatings.

Photograph by April Anson

One of her favorite items in the house is the half-moon-shaped window, which came to her through a twist of fate. Initially she purchased another window for the spot, but soon realized it had some water damage. In a stroke of luck, April was able to find a replacement window that same day for only $30; it fit the rough opening perfectly. The window became one of her favorite features of her home. ⬟

Photograph by April Anson

JAMIE, WENDY, AVERY, & GABE
BARRINGTON

TINY HOUSE ON WHEELS

- VICTOR, COLORADO
- 220 SQUARE FEET
- COMPLETED IN 2014

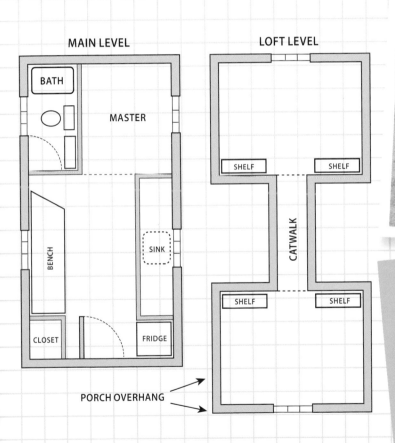

MAIN LEVEL

- BATH
- MASTER
- BENCH
- SINK
- CLOSET
- FRIDGE

LOFT LEVEL

- SHELF
- SHELF
- CATWALK
- SHELF
- SHELF

PORCH OVERHANG

"It's a wonderful thing despite all the test of the will."

Utilities

Electricity: Grid

Heating/Cooling: LG mini split

Water: Well

Water Heating: Propane on demand

Stove: Propane RV and microwave

Refrigeration: 10.72 cubic foot refrigerator

Toilet: Thetford RV

Internet: None

IN 2011 WENDY AND JAMIE BARRINGTON LOST THEIR 2,600-SQUARE-FOOT HOME to foreclosure due to the recession. For a family of four including their sixteen-year-old daughter and eleven-year-old son, you wouldn't think that a tiny home of 220 square feet would be enough, but for the Barringtons it was a dream.

During the build the family had moved into a 1,600-square-foot apartment, then later a 1,000-square-foot apartment as they built their tiny home on nights and weekends. With each downsizing the family decluttered their home and minimized their possessions. They were tired of throwing away money on rent and wanted to get back to a place where they could pursue their dreams, moving to Colorado. The tiny house is the key to that.

Photograph by Wendy Barrington

Photograph by Wendy Barrington

Over eight months the family built their tiny home, mainly led by Jamie, who has been a carpenter for twenty-five years. Because he had the skill and the tools, Jamie was able to do all the work himself except for the welding of the trailer, which they hired a welder to do.

The trailer was an old one that Jamie had from many years before. It needed to be reinforced and new components added in order to get it ready for the tiny house build. For the house, much of the wood came from two main sources: the leftover scraps of a large home Wendy's brother had built, and wood reclaimed from jobs Jamie worked on when he did remodels.

The flooring of their tiny home was built from the leftovers of flooring from the large home of Wendy's brother. During their build, Jamie had remodeled a nearly brand-new condo. Even though it was only a few years old, the owners wanted to gut the whole kitchen. That night Jamie came home with a flawless black marble countertop, which made its way into the tiny house for their kitchen. They reclaimed insulation from job sites and reused it in the house. However, they bought most of the framing and sheathing new.

Photographs by Wendy Barrington

In addition to job sites on which Jamie worked, the couple spent hours scouring Craigslist to find lumber and other objects that would go into their home. At the Habitat for Humanity Restore they were able to find much of the electrical components, bathroom lighting, and all six of their windows, which were bought early on and informed their design. They found some old wood fence panels on the side of the road, which they cleaned up and turned into their interior wall paneling.

In their searching, the Barringtons also relied heavily on word of mouth and talked to lots of people beyond just their friends and family. They shared what they were looking for on Facebook, and soon their work paid off.

Wendy commented that you have to be very persistent when it comes to sites such as Craigslist. Things get posted on the site every day; be ready to hop into the car to get it before someone else can. While shopping in ReStore or similar stores, don't be scared to really dig through bins. The objects there are often dirty, but look for the potential behind the grime. For construction sites, make sure you ask permission before taking anything. Many contractors will freely give you scraps or leftovers rather than pay to dispose of them.

Once you get the reclaimed materials, Wendy suggests, realize that there is going to be a lot of labor to clean them up. Set up an assembly line and get friends and family involved. Many hands make the work go faster. In general the process is: disassemble the items into their base parts, choose the good parts, remove (cut off) any bits that aren't useable, remove nails and screws, use a wire brush to clean up the materials, and then store them for later use.

Photograph by Wendy Barrington

After months of scrounging materials and building their tiny house, the Barringtons moved in early 2014 and have been living there ever since. As a member of a family in only 230 square feet, Wendy shares that "it's daunting sometimes, but I've learned it's a state of mind. You have problems in a big house just as much as in a small one. It's just your perspective and how you deal with it."

While it's tough at times, Wendy and Jamie love their tiny home and how their family gets along in it. The one thing Jamie and Wendy want is for their family to be close. In a tiny house "it comes true, because you can't help but be close. It's a wonderful thing despite all the test of the will. To do this with your family is the greatest thing." ⬟

STACEY'S AIRSTREAM

1992 AIRSTREAM SOVEREIGN

- CALIFORNIA
- 200 SQUARE FEET
- COMPLETED IN 2015

"This is how you're meant to live your whole life!"

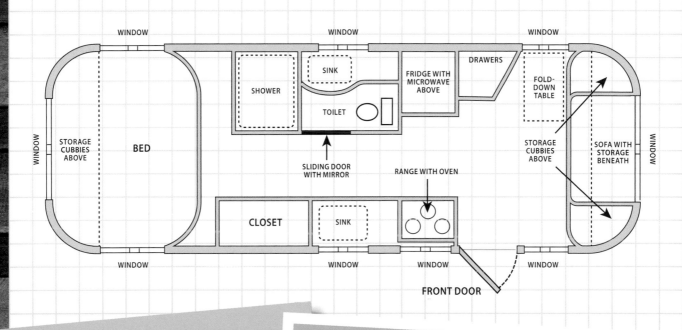

Floor plan labels: WINDOW · SHOWER · SINK · FRIDGE WITH MICROWAVE ABOVE · DRAWERS · FOLD-DOWN TABLE · TOILET · STORAGE CUBBIES ABOVE · BED · STORAGE CUBBIES ABOVE · SOFA WITH STORAGE BENEATH · SLIDING DOOR WITH MIRROR · RANGE WITH OVEN · CLOSET · SINK · FRONT DOOR

Utilities

Electricity: Solar and grid power

Heating/Cooling: Standard Airstream unit

Water: Grid and off-grid capable

Water Heating: Electric and propane

Stove: Propane with oven

Refrigeration: Dometic brand electric/propane unit

Toilet: RV flush, connected to grid

Internet: Shared

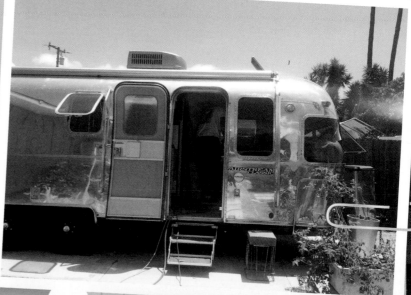

THE FIRST TIME STACEY KNEW THAT SOMETHING HAD TO CHANGE WAS WHEN she found herself shopping on weekends for the sake of filling her large house. She realized that she "wanted to shift, to live more simply." "I'm a single person living in a three-bedroom, two-bathroom house—why do I need all this space?" she asked herself.

Photograph by rawrestorations.com

Photographs by rawrestorations.com

Something about Airstreams has always appealed to her. She looked forward to the day when she could travel the roads with her trailer in tow, seeking adventures. In the immediate period, though, the small space of the trailer would also provide a nice answer to the problem of living in a home that no longer met her needs.

When Stacey first started her journey to convert her Airstream trailer into a place that she would soon call home, her friends and family became worried. As she began to tell her friends what she was doing their response was, "Stace, call me any time if you need to talk." Her stepmother was almost tearful, asking, "Why are you moving into a trailer? Why are you doing this?"

It left Stacey unsure of her path. "I honestly thought I was going to have a panic attack," she says. But she moved forward, knowing this was going to challenge her. If nothing else, she would see if she could live in the Airstream for the summer. After the first week of living in her new home things just seemed right. She began to wonder, "How could I ever live in a big house again?"

Stacey's dad and stepmother made a last-ditch effort to persuade her not to do this. They were so concerned over her new Airstream-trailer life that they called her sister, Carrie, who is Stacey's "voice of reason." They told Carrie, "You've got to get a hold of this! You've got to talk her out of this!" Her sister came over and "started to freak out. She said this is how you're meant to live your whole life!" It was then Stacey began to realize how perfect it really was for her.

Photographs by rawrestorations.com

Photograph by rawrestorations.com

Over time Stacey began to invite her skeptics over for dinners and to hang out. She would invite them in, and in short order they changed their minds. They went from being "really worried for me to, oh my gosh, I totally get it!"

When Stacey first bought the used 1992 trailer it felt very "sterile," and she instantly knew that she wanted to bring in elements of warmth to the space. She chose barn wood to ground the space, adding a cabin feel to it so it could start to feel like a place she could call home.

Photograph by rawrestorations.com

She worked with most of the existing elements of the original Airstream trailer but added accent pieces to the surfaces. Some parts she replaced altogether. The countertops of the kitchenette were replaced with bamboo plywood. She had contractors install the barn wood as flooring and accent walls, and she worked to rehab parts of the trailer that needed some attention including new upholstery and the addition of a fold-out tabletop for meals.

All of her reclaimed wood came from a friend's company called R.A.W. Restorations (rawrestorations.com); it was reclaimed from an old barn in Utah. What resonated deeply with Stacey was the company's goal to preserve and repurpose parts of history. She liked the idea that the story of past things would be carried on in her trailer, creating a new chapter for them. ⬟

MAKAYLA CAVANAGH

TINY HOUSE ON WHEELS

- EASTERN WASHINGTON
- 144 SQUARE FEET
- COMPLETED IN 2015

"It's really disappointing what construction companies will throw away, but it was great for me."

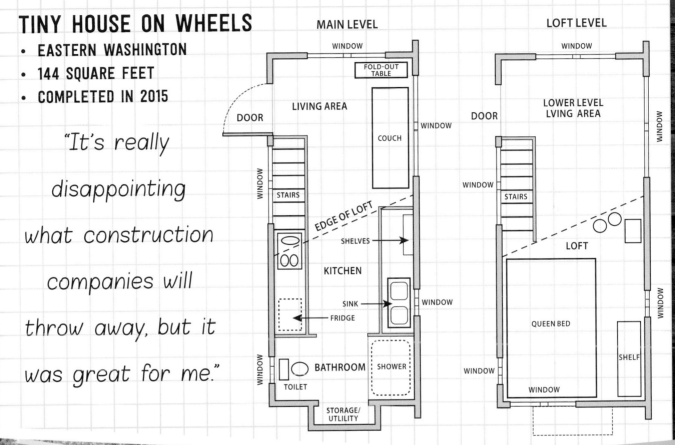

MAIN LEVEL

WINDOW
FOLD-OUT TABLE
DOOR
LIVING AREA
COUCH
WINDOW
WINDOW
STAIRS
EDGE OF LOFT
SHELVES
KITCHEN
SINK
FRIDGE
WINDOW
WINDOW
BATHROOM
SHOWER
TOILET
STORAGE/UTLILITY

LOFT LEVEL

WINDOW
DOOR
LOWER LEVEL LVING AREA
WINDOW
WINDOW
STAIRS
LOFT
QUEEN BED
SHELF
WINDOW
WINDOW

Utilities

Electricity: 30-amp plug-in

Heating/Cooling: Envi heater, ceiling fan

Water: Hose hookup

Water Heating: Eccotemp FVI12

Stove: Wedgewood 3-burner stovetop

Refrigeration: Mini-fridge

Toilet: Nature's Head composting toilet

Internet: None

AFTER RETURNING FROM VOLUNTEERING ABROAD,

Makayla Cavanagh found herself looking for direction. She was trying to figure out what was next when she landed on building a tiny house. The mobility of a tiny house meant that she could move and take her home with her, and the size meant she didn't have to work the rest of her life to pay a mortgage.

To Makayla building a house was unlike anything she had ever done before, but in her mind it was something that she just had to figure out, not something she couldn't do. She remarked that "you can't be afraid to make mistakes," and for her, knowing that she had the support of her friends and family helped.

Photograph by Jessica Humiston

She comes from a family of craftspeople: Her mother is a machinist, and her father works in construction. For her house she was able to get about half her framing lumber from a job site on which her father worked. The lumber was going to be thrown out as scrap. Makayla encourages people to consider looking to construction sites for scrap wood, saying, "It's really disappointing what construction companies will throw away, but it was great for me."

Photograph by Jessica Humiston

Her flooring came from an old building in downtown Spokane, WA. In all, it took her three days of cleaning and resurfacing to get the wood ready for installation. In the end it was worth it; the floors are her favorite part of her house.

Some of her siding and all of her roofing came from a decommissioned military building that was being torn down. She had seen an ad on Craigslist and picked up enough wood to cover her roof and provide accent pieces for the siding. The rest of her siding came from a local reclaimed store. Despite it already being de-nailed, it still took a lot of work to get ready because the boards were badly warped.

Her kitchen and much of her storage was built from a mixture of furniture pieces from the ReStore and scraps she found online. One of her countertops was an old wood door that she spent two days resurfacing. In the end she had a beautiful kitchen nestled underneath her loft.

There were a few items that she wanted to purchase new. To her it was important to have a solid foundation and invest dollars where it mattered. With this in mind she purchased a brand-new trailer on which to build her house. All of her electrical and plumbing fixtures were new so she didn't have to worry about dangers resulting from used electrical components or leaky plumbing parts.

Now that her build is done, Makayla is very happy living in her tiny house. In total the house took less than a year and $13,000 to build. Throughout the process Makayla learned a lot about herself and has inspired others to build tiny houses through her example. It was a lot of work, but in the end she is glad to be living tiny. ⬟

KATE FOX & ANDY GILL

TINY HOUSE ON WHEELS

- PEMBROKESHIRE, UNITED KINGDOM
- 96 SQUARE FEET
- COMPLETED IN 2013

"There are so many materials around and they all have their own stories to tell."

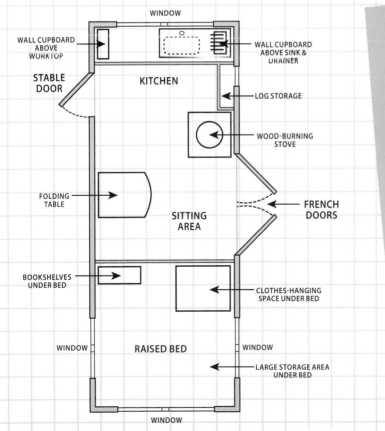

WINDOW

WALL CUPBOARD ABOVE WORKTOP

WALL CUPBOARD ABOVE SINK & DRAINER

STABLE DOOR

KITCHEN

LOG STORAGE

WOOD-BURNING STOVE

FOLDING TABLE

SITTING AREA

FRENCH DOORS

BOOKSHELVES UNDER BED

CLOTHES-HANGING SPACE UNDER BED

WINDOW

RAISED BED

WINDOW

LARGE STORAGE AREA UNDER BED

WINDOW

Utilities

Electricity: 12V solar system: 240W panel, 90AH battery, 12V lights, 350W inverter

Heating/Cooling: Wood-burning stove

Water: Jerry can and 12V pump

Water Heating: Wood-burning stove

Stove: Wood-burning

Refrigeration: Lidded crate under hut

Toilet: None

Internet: 3G mobile Wi-Fi

KATE FOX AND ANDY GILL (KATEFOXMICROHOLDING.CO.UK) ARE NO STRANGERS TO LIVING IN SMALL SPACES. They traveled all over Britain in vans and campers, tending to farms, until they decided to settle down and buy a home. But the couple soon realized that owning a traditional home didn't reflect the life they wanted to live.

Photograph by Kate Fox

Photograph by Kate Fox

"We asked ourselves, why are we living in a box in a town, doing the things we're told we should do like go to work and pay bills, when what we actually did was go off in our camper van and use our house as a great big cupboard for keeping our stuff," Kate says. They sold the house and decided to design and build their own tiny home on wheels.

The couple took their inspiration from old railway cars and shepherd's huts, wagons used by sheepherders in the United Kingdom to follow their flocks. Then, they went to a camper showroom to step inside the small spaces and get a sense of how to lay out their new home. They took those ideas and incorporated them into their own floor plan. By keeping the design simple, Kate and Andy enjoyed a quick building process. It took them two months to get the structure to a point where they could live in it, so they could take their time working on the final details.

Photograph by Kate Fox

Kate has experience with tools, and Andy is a builder by trade, so between them they could tackle the project. Not that it was always easy—making the curved roof was a challenge. They made their own beams using reclaimed wood from an old stable. They had to de-nail it, saw it all down into strips, and glue it all back together again in a curved shape. They spent six weeks on the rafters alone.

Kate and Andy wanted their house to be as sustainable as possible. To do this, they used as much free and salvaged lumber as they could, and took the time to clean it up. A friend gave them some Victorian-era floorboards, and Kate worked for four days with a drill and a wire brush attachment to get them looking like new again. Andy found some old wood from a job site where he was helping to build a barn, and they used those timbers for the studs in the walls. The kitchen is made of old wine crates from all over Europe, which adds a touch of whimsy to the hut. This is one reason why Kate loves working with reclaimed materials. "There are so many materials around and they all have their own stories to tell."

Kate and Andy move their hut every six weeks so they can legally live in it full time, according to UK laws. Since they're always on the move, they chose not to include a toilet or shower inside the hut. There are always facilities wherever they park, whether it's a campsite or a farm. They also have a homemade shower and composting toilet they can set up to use outdoors if they're situated closer to the wilderness.

Photograph by Kate Fox

The couple loves their new home that allows them to move from place to place. They encourage people who are excited about small living to take the leap and just begin, because your energy is really what makes it fun and possible. "If you're enthusiastic and excited, you'll find a way, and everybody's way will be different." ⬟

Photograph by Kate Fox

JAMES GALLETLY

TINY HOUSE ON WHEELS

- CRESCENT HEAD, NEW SOUTH WALES, AUSTRALIA
- 52 SQUARE FEET
- COMPLETED IN 2014

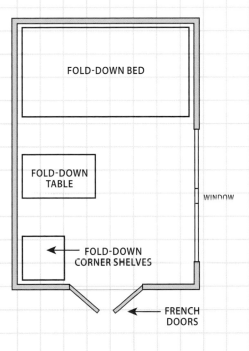

FOLD-DOWN BED

FOLD-DOWN TABLE

WINDOW

FOLD-DOWN CORNER SHELVES ←

FRENCH DOORS ←

Utilities

Electricity: Solar

Heating/Cooling: None

Water: None

Water Heating: None

Stove: None

Refrigeration: None

Toilet: None

Internet: None

"I enjoy the interaction between letting the materials dictate the outcome and working with what you're given."

JAMES GALLETLY WAS VISITING A FRIEND IN CALIFORNIA WHEN HE FIRST PICKED UP A BOOK by tiny house publishing legend Lloyd Kahn. "The biggest part of the appeal is the DIY mentality," he says. "People are building their own homes and coming up with designs that are far more original and creative and have more personality than what is normally considered a home." He took the tiny house idea with him back to his native Australia.

Photograph by Alicia Fox Photography, *www.aliciafoxphotography.com*

Photograph by Alicia Fox Photography, www.aliciafoxphotography.com

James had plenty of experience with straw bale and other natural building techniques, but he had never built a tiny house before. He approached a local rebuilding center and asked them to sponsor the tiny house as a demonstration project. They gave him first pick of the reclaimed materials in stock along with space to work right outside the building. They auctioned off the tiny house once it was finished. The goal of the project was to raise awareness of how recycled materials can be used to reduce building waste and create a beautiful living space.

The design of the tiny caravan depended on the materials at hand. "I enjoyed the creative process. I enjoy the interaction between letting the materials dictate the outcome and working with what you're given," he says. James visited other salvage yards and went dumpster diving to supplement the things he found at the rebuilding center. He spent a month collecting materials before he started building and kept looking for things throughout the rest of the build.

He also reached out to the community in an unconventional way. Next to the tiny house, he had a blackboard where he could write down the things he needed for the project. People from the neighborhood would come by and drop off their extra materials for him to use. One day, James needed insulation and wrote it on the blackboard and shared a photo on social media. He came back the next morning to find piles of insulation left for him inside the half-finished building.

James found a stack of 200 flooring samples at the rebuilding center. He dug through to pick out his favorites, which are used as the interior paneling. A fold-down table and some corner shelves are made from Tasmanian oak cabinet doors. A patchwork of colorful sheets of corrugated metal, reminiscent of a quilt, make up the exterior cladding. He laid all the sheets on the ground, decided which colors looked nice together, and carefully arranged them on the wall for the most pleasing composition.

The French doors were a favorite find. All he had to do was sand them down and finish them with tung oil to bring them back to life. He had trouble finding the perfect door handles to complete the look and was about to go out and buy something new. Minutes later, someone came into the rebuilding center to donate the perfect hardware, and James snapped it up!

The few materials bought new included the house wrap, the electrical wiring, and the nails and screws. James estimates that 95 percent of the tiny house is built with reclaimed materials. He advises builders looking to use secondhand materials to keep an open mind and creatively use the things you find along the way. "It's the most enjoyable part about secondhand materials. It's so much easier to work with the textures and the palette you're given." ⬟

Photographs by Alicia Fox Photography, www.aliciafoxphotography.com

TINY HALL HOUSE

TINY HOUSE ON WHEELS

- GREATER BOSTON AREA, MASSACHUSETTS
- 196 SQUARE FEET
- COMPLETED IN 2014

MAIN LEVEL

- SHOWER
- BATHROOM
- SINK
- KITCHEN & CLOSETS
- CLOSET
- COUNTER & STOVE
- DROP-LEAF DESK
- LIVING ROOM
- DROP-LEAF DESK
- COUCH WITH STORAGE UNDER
- FRONT DOOR

LOFT LEVEL

- QUEEN-SIZED BED
- STAIRS

"Evaluating every single object in your life forces you to deal with what's actually important in your life."

Utilities

Electricity: One 15-amp circuit (house runs on less than 1200W)

Heating/Cooling: Envi panel, 400W; Aeratron AE3 ceiling fan

Water: 48-gallon on-board water tank with water inlet via hose

Water Heating: PrecisionTemp RV-550 propane on demand

Stove: Convection Fagor single-burner

Refrigeration: Frigidaire, Compact Energy Star

Toilet: Airhead composting toilet

Internet: Wi-Fi hot spot

THE HALL FAMILY HAD BEEN THINKING OF BUYING THE BOSTON-AREA TOWNHOUSE THEY WERE RENTING, but the real-estate prices were sky-high. They knew of tiny houses and loved the idea of living small with just the things they needed, so they sold their stuff, settled on a design, and dove right into the building process.

They didn't have much building experience, but with a lot of research and the help of friends, they were able to build the house in six months. It was important to them that they built the house as a family, with their teenage son taking part in the build. The Internet made it easy to find solutions to problems as they arose. "There were very few things we couldn't look up," they said.

Photographs by A. Hall; photograph on opposite page by A. Hall

The Hall family wanted their house to be as sustainable and nontoxic as possible. They used as many reclaimed, handmade, unprocessed, and locally sourced materials as they could. "The whole point of the tiny house was to align our political and social beliefs with how we were actually living," they said. Their front door is a reclaimed 100-year-old Mission-style door, which took a lot of time and money to restore—but it's made of solid wood, and there's no off-gassing. Other things were free; the drawer pulls in their kitchen came from a collection of beach rocks.

Photographs by A. Hall

The family spent hundreds of hours digging through salvage yards to find diamonds in the rough. They found three handmade brass hinges with acorn details for $40, a fraction of the cost to buy them new. But they were grimy and covered in paint, and it took weeks to clean them. The stained-glass window in the bathroom door was another salvage yard find. It was in great shape, but it was stuck in a moldy wooden frame. Getting the frame off the window without breaking the glass was a challenge!

Photographs by A. Hall

For the Halls, putting in the work to get the best-quality materials was worth it, but sometimes it was difficult to find items that they needed. At one point, they bought a porch light from Home Depot because they couldn't find a light they liked at an affordable price. Then they found one that was even better on Craigslist, snatched it up, and quickly returned the original light to the store. They also found a brass bar stool footrest in a salvage bin and dug through every hardware barrel in the store until they found three more. The footrests now hold the bed in place in the loft.

Photographs by A. Hall

The Halls were deliberate in their approach to getting rid of their excess clutter. They picked their favorite books to keep and digitized many of the rest before donating them. All of their photos, movies, and music are now stored on two hard drives. They hosted "Craigslist days" where they invited people to come through their house and buy the things they wanted. Each member of the family got a memory box, and whatever mementos they wanted to keep had to fit in their box. Everything else was donated or given away. They advise that you take a lot of time—six months to a year—to get rid of your unneeded things. "The experience of evaluating every single object in your life really forces you to deal with what's actually important in your life."

After months of hard work the house was done, and as they moved into the home the family agreed that if anyone was unhappy with living in the tiny house, they would find a different place to live and the house could be a vacation home. The house was an experiment for the family, but they were excited to live in it together. A year later everyone has loved living in the home the entire family built. ⬠

Photograph by A. Hall

SARAH HASTINGS

TINY HOUSE ON WHEELS

- WESTERN MASSACHUSETTS
- 190 SQUARE FEET
- COMPLETED IN 2015

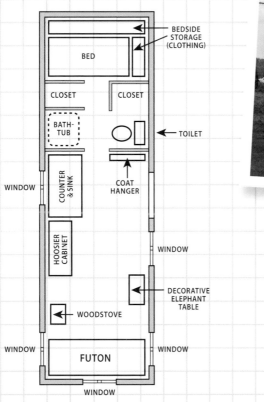

Floor plan labels: BEDSIDE STORAGE (CLOTHING), BED, CLOSET, CLOSET, BATH-TUB, TOILET, WINDOW, COUNTER & SINK, COAT HANGER, HOOSIER CABINET, WINDOW, DECORATIVE ELEPHANT TABLE, WOODSTOVE, WINDOW, WINDOW, FUTON, WINDOW, WINDOW

Utilities

Electricity: Grid and solar

Heating/Cooling: Morso 1410 woodstove; ceiling fan

Water: Hose hookup and tank

Water Heating: Stiebel Eltron on-demand water heater

Stove: Extra-wide toaster oven, hot plate, and microwave

Refrigeration: Mini-fridge

Toilet: Homemade humanure (composting) toilet with separate buckets for liquids and solids

Internet: None

"Don't overly romanticize the building process. It's mentally and physically exhausting. But it's totally possible."

SARAH HAD ALWAYS DREAMED OF BUILDING HER OWN HOUSE. She discovered tiny houses online during her freshman year of college while researching sustainable homes. Her own tiny house would later become her senior year thesis project to complete her architecture degree. In July 2014 Sarah bought a twenty-seven-foot-long gooseneck trailer and dove right into the build. Working mostly on weekends with friends and family to help, she finished the house a year later.

Sarah built only with materials found within a 200-mile radius of her building location. Even the structural insulated panels (SIPs) she used to construct the walls were manufactured in New Hampshire.

Sarah chose the SIPs because of their strength, ease of use, and high insulation value. She decided to keep the electrical components on the surface of the interior walls in case she ever needed to fix them. The exposed conduit lends the house an industrial look.

Many of the fittings and finishes in Sarah's house are reclaimed. All of her windows are used—two of them had a previous life in a library. The siding on the gable ends of her house came from a recent renovation of the Springfield, MA, fire station, and the siding on the long sides of the house she found at a junkyard. Her front door is a midcentury modern style from the 1960s.

Photograph by Sarah G. Hastings

Photograph by Sarah G. Hastings

Sarah's new bamboo flooring was left over from a friend's project, and it was just enough to cover the whole floor. Even her kitchen sink is reclaimed—it came from a dentist's office.

Freestanding furniture makes Sarah's house feel more like a home. Her Hoosier cabinet was a Craigslist find purchased from a woman with a house full of antiques. The piece is the first thing you see when you walk in the door. "They're on Craigslist all the time, because they were made in high quantities in the 1920s, 1930s, and 1940s," Sarah says. The Hoosier cabinet is a great solution for Sarah's kitchen, because it has lots of storage and even features pull-out counter space.

The timber trusses that support the roof are the centerpiece of the house. They're crafted from 100-year-old reclaimed wood salvaged from a factory that was part of the oldest furniture-making company in the United States. Tom Musco at Royalston Oak Custom Timber Frames donated a lot of his time to help her and her father build the frames. The timbers add a lot of color and texture to the home, and they still feature the original nail holes. They add a unique character that you can't find in many tiny houses.

Sarah suggests assembling a support system of more experienced builders before you start your tiny house project. "Don't overly romanticize the building process," she says. "It's mentally and physically exhausting. But it's totally possible." She also advises prospective tiny house builders to treat all challenges and obstacles as puzzles to be solved rather than roadblocks.

Photograph by Sarah G. Hastings

She hopes that other tiny house builders will build their houses to reflect their own local culture and the places where they build. She also thinks that the merging of old and new—historical inspiration and modern technology—is what can make a tiny house truly special. ⬟

ZEE KESLER

TINY HOUSE ON WHEELS

- VANCOUVER, BRITISH COLUMBIA
- 158 SQUARE FEET
- COMPLETED IN 2015

"When people see something interesting, they just want to be part of it—that's art."

Utilities

Electricity: 110V and 220V hookup options

Heating/Cooling: Space heater

Water: Hose hookup

Water Heating: None

Stove: None

Refrigeration: None

Toilet: None

Internet: None

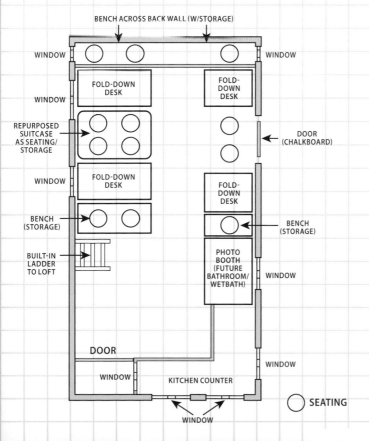

BENCH ACROSS BACK WALL (W/STORAGE)

WINDOW

WINDOW

REPURPOSED SUITCASE AS SEATING/ STORAGE

WINDOW

BENCH (STORAGE)

BUILT-IN LADDER TO LOFT

FOLD-DOWN DESK

FOLD-DOWN DESK

FOLD-DOWN DESK

WINDOW

DOOR (CHALKBOARD)

FOLD-DOWN DESK

BENCH (STORAGE)

PHOTO BOOTH (FUTURE BATHROOM/ WETBATH)

WINDOW

DOOR

WINDOW

KITCHEN COUNTER

WINDOW

WINDOW

◯ SEATING

ZEE KESLER LIVES IN VANCOUVER, CANADA, A CITY THAT
RECENTLY ACHIEVED the doubtful distinction of having the highest cost of
living in North America. It is also in the top twenty for the most expensive places to
live in the world. With the city continuing to grow, tiny houses are one solution to
urban infill that could help bring some affordable options to the city.

While most tiny houses are designed to live in, Zee saw the potential for other uses.
While the house could be used as a home with a few modifications, it initially started
out as a mobile classroom and mini art gallery.

Photograph by Erin Leigh Pasternak, www.erinpasternak.com

Photograph by Erin Leigh Pasternak, *www.erinpasternak.com*

With the house now complete Zee admits that while it's a great focal point of learning and art, it "brings up conversations of affordable housing without it being the mission." Zee says that in her own way she is able to spark conversations about the rising cost of living, explaining "that the artist's job is not to directly address issues but divert the conversation."

Starting out Zee didn't really know too much about building, but she was very good at enlisting help and support. She spent the first year of her journey collecting materials, often spending twenty to thirty hours a week at it. Every time she found a lead on some materials that could be reclaimed she had to borrow or rent a car because she didn't own one.

She did have a place to keep all the collected items; her landlord didn't use the garage so she was able store all the materials that later would become a house there. From the beginning Zee made many key choices about her systems: heating, cooling, water, power, and appliances.

Once she had her systems selected she built a design from the outside in. Because the tiny house needed to be mobile, there were requirements for how wide it could be. This led her to design the house starting at the outermost edge and working toward the center of the home to make sure she fit with the necessary parameters.

With her design finalized Zee and her designer were able to make a list of what lumber they would need, from which she developed her "cut list." This was a list of each board they'd need and how long it should be. This list proved to be very valuable when evaluating materials; if an item could be used for something on their list, then they'd take it; otherwise they'd decline.

Photograph by Erin Leigh Pasternak, www.erinpasternak.com

Photograph by Erin Leigh Pasternak, *www.erinpasternak.com*

Saying no was a big lesson Zee learned early on. There are times when people want you to take all their materials. Sometimes, since you drove out to check what people have, they'll guilt you into saying yes. The downside of taking things you don't need is that you'll later have to give them away or worse, pay to have them disposed of.

Zee quickly learned this lesson and began to collect only what she needed. Each time she found something on her cut list, she would de-nail it, cut it to rough dimensions, and stack it on her storage racks.

The storage racks were something Zee wishes she had done sooner. At first they tried piling things neatly but soon it got unwieldy. Once she erected the racks, she piled her pieces of wood in reverse order of when she would need them. The result was that as they built, the board on top was most often the next board she needed for that part of the house.

With all the materials in place the house took about six months to build. Her team of volunteers and paid contractors came together around the inspiring idea that Zee had envisioned. Her team—John McFarlane (designer), Josh Armstrong (carpenter), Dave Myers (carpenter), Nathyn Sanche (welder), David Heck (volunteer builder), Shauna Langfield (volunteer builder), Ben Garratt (building and assistance with electrical), Tom Ferguson (volunteer builder), and Ruth Munro (artist)—all worked to build the house.

In all, the house cost $25,000 Canadian to build. It now serves as a public art piece, classroom, and gallery all in one tiny space. It's currently parked at the Trout Lake Community Centre as part of their Artists in Communities program. The build would have never happened without the community rallying around the idea of the tiny house. Zee says, "When people see something interesting, they just want to be part of it—that's art." ⬟

Photograph by Erin Leigh Pasternak, www.erinpasternak.com

AARON MARET

TINY HOUSE ON WHEELS

- TRAVELING ACROSS THE U.S.
- 196 SQUARE FEET
- COMPLETED IN 2013

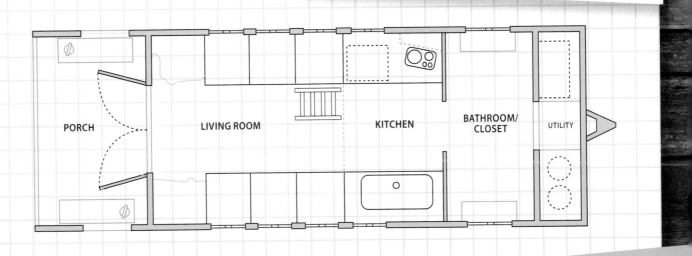

PORCH　　LIVING ROOM　　KITCHEN　　BATHROOM/CLOSET　　UTILITY

"The whole process—the research, the design, and the actual construction of it—was one of my favorite things I've ever done."

Utilities

Electricity: Wired for dual 100V AC/12V DC

Heating/Cooling: Sig Marine P9000 propane heater

Water: Hose hookup

Water Heating: None

Stove: 2-burner propane drop-in cooktop (Atwood DV-20S)

Refrigeration: 3-way (propane, AC, DC) under-counter refrigerator (Dometic RM2193RB)

Toilet: Custom-built composting toilet cabinet

Internet: None

AARON MARET STARTED HIS CAREER AS AN ARCHITECT, DESIGNING BUILDINGS THAT WOULD LATER be built far away, and he often never saw them once they were completed. Over the years he was drawn to the construction of homes, not just their design. In the end he came across tiny houses when he was building homes. What drew him to tiny houses was the size. In his words a tiny house is "the sweet spot in terms of scale" when it comes to building because he can touch every part of the build. In most of his professional projects he often had help or in some cases work was subcontracted out, but with his tiny house he was able to enjoy the entire process of the build and add his craftsmanship to the project.

Photograph by Aaron Maret

In particular, Aaron loved the fact that due to the small size of the project, it was possible to use reclaimed materials. This wasn't true of larger projects because of the quantity of materials needed. Aaron says, "The whole process—the research, the design, and the actual construction of it—was one of my favorite things I've ever done."

Aaron had a large shop, which made the processing and storage of reclaimed materials much easier. As a builder, he was "always looking for materials" for his projects. He admits that while using reclaimed materials often results in superior finished pieces, it's a lot of work.

For his house's siding he used wood off an old barn, which he was able to purchase in a raw state from a local reclaimed store. He then spent well over 100 hours denailing, jointing, and planing so the boards could later be installed on the outside of the house. As with all the reclaimed materials he used in his house, this process took time, often more than he had planned for. "Take your estimates and times it by three" is Aaron's mantra when it comes to the time investment for reclaimed materials.

Despite all the labor, Aaron says, the attraction of working with older reclaimed wood "is the durability, the quality, and at its heart: honesty. It has so much character, the original saw marks from the milling, and it tells a story that adds a richness. It adds meaning, but it also has warmth."

Photograph by Aaron Maret

Photograph by Aaron Maret

In his home about a third of the framing was reclaimed. Most of the sheathing was salvaged from an art studio and had paint drips and splashes all over it. He thought about keeping that as the siding because it made the house look neat. His door was from a 1920s farmhouse, and a few of his windows came from salvage as well.

There are a few things that he feels shouldn't be reclaimed. "Invest where it matters," Aaron advises. All of his operable windows were brand new, his roof and insulation were bought at the store, and he insisted that all wiring and plumbing should be new.

Photograph by Aaron Maret

Living in the house with his partner and their child was tough at first because they didn't always have the space to be alone when they needed to be. He says that as a family "the process of reducing was iterative. It took session after session and took a remarkable amount of energy to fit into a tiny house." But in the end Aaron's family settled into the tiny house very comfortably, finding nooks where each person could have his space in the small home. ⬟

MARK MILLER

TINY HOUSE ON A FOUNDATION

- GRANTSBURG, WISCONSIN
- 204 SQUARE FEET
- 1920'S SUMMER KITCHEN REMODELED IN 2015

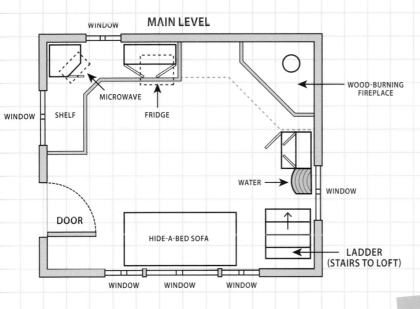

MAIN LEVEL

WINDOW

WINDOW

SHELF

MICROWAVE

FRIDGE

WOOD-BURNING FIREPLACE

WATER →

WINDOW

DOOR

HIDE-A-BED SOFA

LADDER (STAIRS TO LOFT)

WINDOW WINDOW WINDOW

LOFT LEVEL

BED

WINDOW

LADDER (STAIRS TO LOFT)

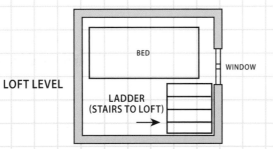

"You really have to be able to see things for what they will be eventually."

Utilities

Electricity: 110-amp service

Heating/Cooling: Wood-burning fireplace, electric baseboard, ceiling fan

Water: Water cooler

Water Heating: Microwave

Stove: Microwave

Refrigeration: Mini-fridge

Toilet: Outdoor porta-potty

Internet: Yes

MARK MILLER HAS BEEN COLLECTING AND USING RECLAIMED MATERIALS ALL HIS LIFE. In his words, "Taking things that most people call junk and turning them into something neat looking is something I enjoy doing." As a contractor he is an experienced builder who loves to work the materials he finds into his build.

Looking toward retirement Mark knew that he would need to be creative, so he started looking for other sources of income. He decided to build a small cabin to move into so he could rent out his larger home, a home that was now too big since his children had grown.

Through his entire build on the cabin he had to be very creative when it came to using what he found. He says, "You really have to be able to see things for what they will be eventually." Much of the wood came from scraps he found while he was driving around the area. He'd stop and put them in his truck and then store them for later. More often than not he'd collect things without knowing what he'd use them for.

The flooring of his cabin came from an old office space. The floors had been installed in 1895. The fireplace was from a dumpster. Much of the dimensional lumber came from trees that had fallen over in his grandmother's yard. He cut them to length and milled them into boards.

Photograph by Mark Miller

Photographs by Mark Miller

Mark shared that he is always on the lookout for materials to use in various projects. He is fortunate to have a large outbuilding in which he can store everything until a need arises. When it comes to working on a project, Mark can look through what he has on hand and most often can find what he needs.

Whenever Mark finds wood, he always asks permission to take it. He never assumes that it's okay to take scrap pieces even if they're in the trash. When he gets permission, Mark says, "I always make sure to leave the site neater than it was when I got there." This good will has landed Mark a lot of great finds, some of which made it into his cabin.

Whenever Mark finds wood for free, he takes it home and immediately de-nails. That way the wood can be stored flat. He told me, "If you leave nails in the board, each board doesn't seat neatly into a pile."

"It's important," says Mark, "to have a good storage space out of the elements." There had been times that he stored wood reclaimed from old buildings and barns under tarps, but he found that even with a good tarp, moisture proves to be a challenge. A solid structure where you can keep materials off the ground is important to prevent lumber from rotting.

Today his cabin sits next to a stream on Mark's property. He loves the small space and the view from the large reclaimed windows overlooking the water. What started out as odds and ends collected over the years came together to build his little cabin. ⬠

Photograph by Mark Miller

DOMINIQUE MOODY

TINY HOUSE ON WHEELS

- LOS ANGELES, CALIFORNIA
- 140 SQUARE FEET
- COMPLETED IN 2015

"It's an art form to create our shelter in reflection of who we are."

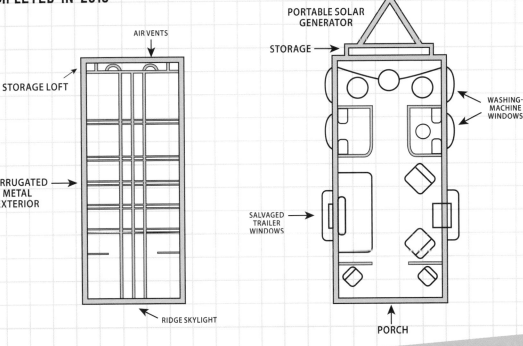

STORAGE LOFT

AIR VENTS

CORRUGATED METAL EXTERIOR

RIDGE SKYLIGHT

PORTABLE SOLAR GENERATOR

STORAGE

WASHING-MACHINE WINDOWS

SALVAGED TRAILER WINDOWS

PORCH

Utilities

Electricity: 12V/110/LED portable solar MC Goal Zero

Heating/Cooling: 12V portable heater and fans

Water: 5-gallon glass carboy/1-gallon stainless steel drinking thermos/2.5-gallon stainless steel shower

Water Heating: Reduction cooktop, thermos storage

Stove: Portable induction cooktop/MaxiMatic 600W

Refrigeration: Avanti Undercounter 12V refrigerator

Toilet: Thetford portable marine biodegradable toilet

Internet: Mobile hot spot

DOMINIQUE MOODY HAS BEEN AN ASSEMBLAGE ARTIST FOR MANY YEARS, making art with found materials. The Nomad is both her home and latest masterpiece. Since the eighties, she had been planning to build a house truck. However, in 2002, she discovered an article about Jay Shafer and his tiny house. After contacting him and learning more, Dominique knew that a tiny house was the perfect medium through which to tell her story.

She is no stranger to the nomadic lifestyle. Her father was in the military, and Dominique was born in Germany. Her family moved around constantly during her childhood, living in a forty-foot New Moon trailer when they returned to the United States. Her current location in Los Angeles is one of forty-five different addresses she's had throughout her life. It turns out she has wanderlust in her blood—her family line can be traced back to an ancient African nomadic tribe, the largest on the planet.

Dominique's tiny house is truly a labor of love. The house took four years to design, and an additional three years to construct. She is legally blind, and built the house with the help of friends, family, volunteers, and hired professionals.

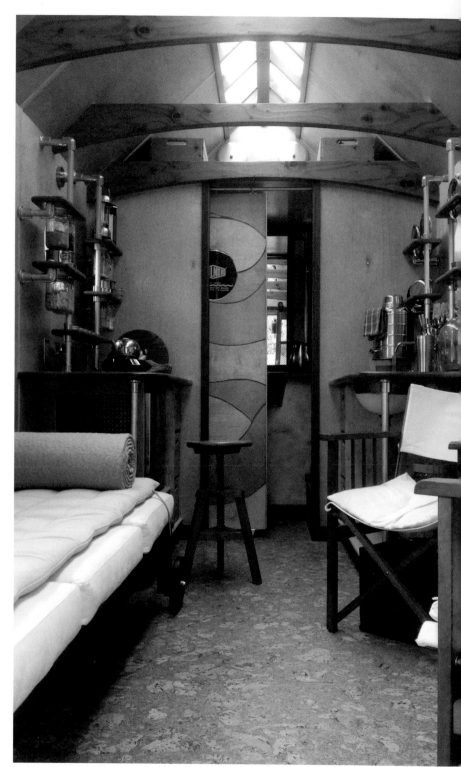

Photograph by Khari Scott and Dominique Moody

Photographs by Khari Scott and Dominique Moody

Because she is partially sighted, she focused on filling the house with round, organic shapes and the textures of wood and metal. The corrugated steel siding of her house isn't reclaimed, but it's striking. Dominique rusted the metal with a mixture of water, vinegar, and salt, and then colored the steel with metal stain.

Dominique knew she wanted round windows in her tiny house, but specialty windows are expensive. One day at the laundromat, she realized the round door on the washing machine looked just like the kind of window she wanted! She found a company that refurbishes old commercial laundry machines, and she was able to get six windows for the price of one round window bought new.

Reclaimed wood adds a variety of stories to the tiny house. Clear heart redwood from 1,500-year-old trees came from a demolished bridge in Bakersfield, CA, and Dominique had used it for an art installation she made for a hospital. She used the leftover redwood as the baseboard, trim for her skylight, and shower surround. Found tree branches work beautifully as hand rails on the porch. The porch itself is clad with 100-year-old barn wood, and the wooden threshold of an old stable, worn down in the center by horse hooves, serves as the lintel above the door. One woman even gifted Dominique ten boxes of cedar paneling, which she used as lining for her kitchen drawers and as the flooring in her storage loft.

Since the house is an art piece reflecting her family history, Dominique made sure that family items were given a place of honor. Her father carried a globe with him wherever he traveled, and it now hangs above the entry in a half-spherical window. His apple crates that once held books became the drawers for her kitchen cabinets. A simple galvanized tub of his is now her bathroom sink, and it is the first thing you see when you walk in the door.

Dominique Moody's tiny house is a living, breathing work of art many years in the making. Not only does it represent the past and present of her story, but it also helps strike up conversations about what it means to create a meaningful home in this day and age. "A place is one thing—a home is a complete other kind of environment," Dominique says. "It's an art form to create our shelter in reflection of who we are." ⬟

Photograph by Khari Scott and Dominique Moody

GREG PARHAM

TINY HOUSE ON WHEELS

- DURANGO, COLORADO
- 161 SQUARE FEET
- COMPLETED IN 2013

"You have to pull nails, you have to scrape off paint, and maybe they're warped or twisted so you fix that."

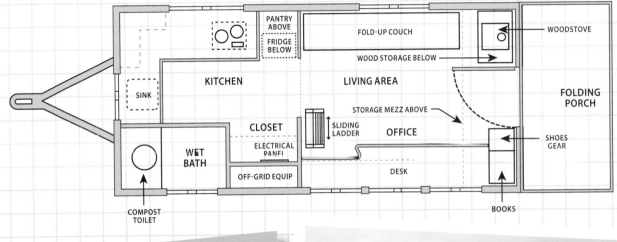

PANTRY ABOVE
FRIDGE BELOW
FOLD-UP COUCH
WOODSTOVE
WOOD STORAGE BELOW
KITCHEN
LIVING AREA
FOLDING PORCH
SINK
STORAGE MEZZ ABOVE
CLOSET
SLIDING LADDER
OFFICE
SHOES GEAR
ELECTRICAL PANEL
WET BATH
OFF-GRID EQUIP
DESK
COMPOST TOILET
BOOKS

Utilities

Electricity: Solar, 12V DC lights and water pump, 100V AC inverter

Heating/Cooling: Woodstove (primary), propane furnace (backup)

Water: 48-gallon freshwater tank with Shurflo pump

Water Heating: Propane on demand

Stove: Propane Camp Chef 2-burner with oven

Refrigeration: 4.5 cubic foot refrigerator

Toilet: Lovable Loo

Internet: Wireless satellite

AFTER MOVING TO DURANGO, CO, IN LATE 2011 GREG PARHAM WAS LOOKING FOR A PLACE TO CALL HOME. He began looking at small lots on which to build a cabin. While looking for land his real-estate agent showed him an article about tiny houses, and he knew he had found the answer to what he was looking for.

Photographs by Rocky Mountain Tiny Houses

Photograph by Rocky Mountain Tiny Houses

The house took him two months working on it part time. During the weekdays he was a contractor working on a construction job. The tiny house he built is the one he lives in today, but he has since gone on to launch a building company called Rocky Mountain Tiny Houses.

Building with reclaimed materials has been a challenge for Greg. He notes that "there just aren't a lot of people around to get stuff from." The small town of Durango has 17,000 people, which makes for slim pickings when it comes to reclaimed materials. As a result it took a long time to gather materials to build the house. Over time he was able to gather much of what he needed, but up to that point, it proved challenging to keep piles from being an eyesore.

Photograph by Rocky Mountain Tiny Houses

Working with reclaimed materials can be much more difficult despite the amazing finished products. To get wood to a usable state, Greg says, "you have to pull nails, you have to scrape off paint, and maybe they're warped or twisted so you have to fix that." It really comes down to a limited budget because "if you're building your own house on your own time, yes, it will be cheaper. But if you have to pay somebody, in the end it's probably going to be more."

For Greg, using reclaimed materials is driven by a mixture of cost and aesthetic. He loves the look and richness reclaimed lumber brings. While sometimes building as a business dictates using new wood purchased from the store, he loves it when he can bring reclaimed elements into his build. Newer lumber, he thinks, doesn't stack up when compared to reclaimed materials. The end product with those materials always turns out better.

Each of the houses he has built has been different; each of them used a variety of reclaimed materials in it. For the house he built for himself, he got the windows from a renovation in which he removed nearly brand-new windows that were being ripped out and replaced. He often uses old corrugated metal roofing panels for siding because of its durability and aesthetic.

In the end Greg has built several tiny homes using reclaimed materials, each one as unique as the parts that go into it. The homes are beautiful, with a mixture of new, used, and upcycled parts. They come together to create warm and inviting spaces. ⬠

Photograph by Rocky Mountain Tiny Houses

NATALIE POLLARD

TINY HOUSE ON WHEELS

- ASHEVILLE, NORTH CAROLINA
- 265 SQUARE FEET
- COMPLETED IN 2014

MAIN LEVEL

- SHOWER
- TOILET
- SINK
- COUNTER
- KITCHEN
- COUNTER
- ARMOIRE CLOSET
- COVERED ENTRY — 8' sliding glass door
- LADDER TO LOFT
- LIVING ROOM
- DAYBED

LOFT LEVEL

8' × 10' LOFT

2' × 2'8" OPEN ENTRANCE

"I made the correlation that less space meant more money, more time, and more freedom."

Utilities

Electricity: Grid

Heating/Cooling: Life Corp infrared space heater, #LS-3ECO

Water: Carried in, no running water

Water Heating: On-demand hot water heater, Rinnai #v53

Stove: Ramblewood 2-burner gas stove, #GC2-48P

Refrigeration: Frigidaire 4.5 cubic foot compact, #FFPE45L2QM

Toilet: Composting toilet by JT Homesteader

Internet: ATT U-Verse

HAVING ONCE OWNED A HOME, NATALIE POLLARD (FORVILLAGERS .COM) KNEW THAT WHEN she moved to Asheville, NC, buying a house didn't appeal to her at all. "The weight and responsibility of owning a home," she says, was too much. Renting, however, had left her searching for a better option. Finally she spoke with a friend who asked, "When were you the happiest? What living situation left you feeling the best?" Natalie spent some time reflecting seriously on the question and came to realize "the point I was really happy in my life was when I lived in really tiny spaces. I made the correlation that less space meant more money, more time, and more freedom." That realization solidified her plans, giving her a direction to move forward. She would live tiny.

She spent time planning her move to a new home, initially thinking about building a yurt. One day, though, she found herself talking with some friends who happened to be builders. Their company is called Nanostead, and they have built small homes for years. Now, though, they wanted to build a tiny house. Natalie offered to be their first client; the perfect option seemed "to just fall into my lap," Natalie says.

Natalie was excited to see her home take shape. The fact that it was built by friends made it feel as if "it had a special quality to it, like a handmade gift." Because the home was being built for her, she had to make a number of decisions when it came to the finishing and design elements.

Photograph by Tamara Gavin; Photograph on opposite page by Max Cooper Photography

Photograph by Tamara Gavin

The house used a lot of reclaimed elements in it, and where the components weren't reclaimed, the builders opted for locally sourced materials. The house was framed, sheathed, and sided with lumber milled by a local family-owned lumber mill. Several accent walls are sided with reclaimed materials from an old cabin built during the Civil War; the cabin had been deconstructed and milled into planks.

Natalie's flooring was from a local salvage store, which captures lumber from construction sites and resells it so it doesn't enter the waste stream. Her counters, storage, and cabinets were all bought at thrift and antique stores and then combined into the various components of her kitchen and storage spaces.

Throughout her house she loved using reclaimed and repurposed materials because many of them had a closeness to her. Some things came from friends and family, adding a sentimental dimension to the elements of her house. Natalie says for those things that came from people she knew she likes "the embodied energy from the materials that comes from time." Some items came from her own store, Villagers, in Asheville, NC (*http://forvillagers .com*).

The final house was exactly what Natalie was looking for. Moving into her home was an adjustment, but she notes that "a well-designed space made it easy." Her new life meant that she was "afforded so much freedom and had so little stress" that she couldn't imagine living any other way. ⬟

GARETH ROBERTS

TINY HOUSE ON WHEELS

- FERNIE, BRITISH COLUMBIA
- 182 SQUARE FEET
- COMPLETED IN 2015

"There's so much waste with construction materials because something isn't absolutely perfect."

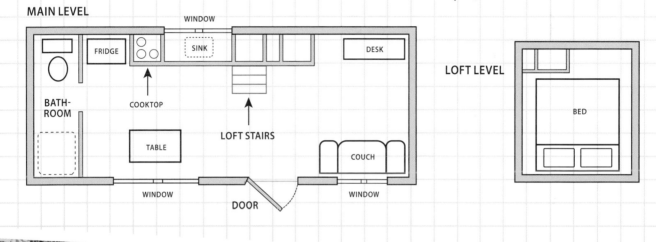

MAIN LEVEL

WINDOW

FRIDGE

SINK

DESK

COOKTOP

LOFT LEVEL

BATH-ROOM

BED

TABLE

LOFT STAIRS

COUCH

WINDOW

DOOR

WINDOW

Utilities

Electricity: 30-amp service

Heating/Cooling: Electric heater and fan

Water: Grid

Water Heating: Atwood 6-gallon propane water heater

Stove: Suburban 3-burner cooktop

Refrigeration: Side-by-side Avanti refrigerator freezer

Toilet: Nature's Head composting toilet

Internet: Wi-Fi

HUMMINGBIRD MICRO HOMES IS A TINY HOUSE COMPANY IN FERNIE, BRITISH COLUMBIA, founded in the spring of 2014. Gareth Roberts is one of the cofounders and head builders at the company. Gareth had built a tiny home for his sister-in-law a year prior, and this experiment in building and design turned into a thriving business. Hummingbird is a two-man building team that focuses on building tiny houses with creativity and thoughtful intention.

Photograph by Hummingbird Micro Homes

Photograph by Hummingbird Micro Homes

Photograph by Hummingbird Micro Homes

Gareth used to work in conventional construction, but now he likes to follow what he calls "the emerging process" of building. He starts with the blank slate of a tiny house frame, then designs the house as he finds secondhand materials. The form, size, and shape of the wood he uses often dictates and guides the final design. It's a unique perspective for a tiny house building company. Gareth says it's time consuming but economical to find materials this way. "Everything's already out there. Somebody's got a pile of something in their backyard they want to get rid of," he says. "You just have to commit to going around on weekends to find stuff."

Gareth mostly finds materials on the side of the road, so he's learned to keep his eyes open. He also has a "borderline addiction" to Kijiji, the Canadian equivalent of Craigslist—and he doesn't limit himself to local listings. He once drove twenty-six hours to pick up a woodstove and also got a mini cast-iron claw-foot bathtub out of the deal. He suggests doing research and knowing how much things cost, so you can determine what's worth your time and more easily spot a deal.

One of the company's newest tiny house models, the Cowboy, features all kinds of reclaimed materials. The reclaimed lumber siding was a roadside find. Gareth was driving when he spotted a pile of lumber in someone's front yard. The wood had been left outside for years, and most of it was unusable. He had to sort through the pile for the best pieces, but the owner let him have the lumber for free. The rest of the siding is made up of recycled metal.

The kitchen cabinets in the Cowboy were converted from old found wooden boxes. The kitchen sink was found at a secondhand store (Gareth says that stainless steel sinks are great to find secondhand, because there are so many of them). The windows are reclaimed, and even though they're different shapes and sizes, they look cohesive when paired with the contemporary exterior. Most of the interior bamboo wall covering and pine tongue-and-groove ceiling are reclaimed too, and the different colors add a lot of texture to the inside of the house.

Photograph by Hummingbird Micro Homes

Gareth says it's easy to find things if you're willing to take the time. He treats the hunt for reclaimed materials like a job and dedicates a little time every day to hunt for treasure online or out in the community. "There's so much waste with construction materials because something isn't absolutely perfect," he says. If you put in the work to find those slightly imperfect but completely useable secondhand materials, you can have a tiny home filled with much more beauty and character. ⬟

CONRAD ROGUE

TINY HOUSE ON FOUNDATION

- JACKSONVILLE, OREGON
- 70 SQUARE FEET
- COMPLETED IN 2013

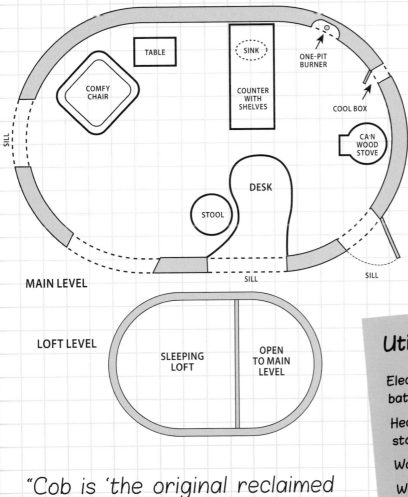

TABLE

COMFY CHAIR

SINK

ONE-PIT BURNER

COUNTER WITH SHELVES

COOL BOX

SILL

CA'N WOOD STOVE

DESK

STOOL

MAIN LEVEL

SILL

SILL

LOFT LEVEL

SLEEPING LOFT

OPEN TO MAIN LEVEL

"Cob is 'the original reclaimed material. Energetically it gives a very nice feel.'"

Utilities

Electricity: 50W solar panel and small battery

Heating/Cooling: Olive oil candles and tiny can stove

Water: 3-gallon carboy (rain water)

Water Heating: None

Stove: Single-burner can stove

Refrigeration: Cool box on the north side of the cob wall

Toilet: None

Internet: None

CONRAD ROGUE IS NOT NEW TO BUILDING SPACES FOR
HIMSELF. Early on in life he bought some land and built a small cabin, and from
that he began a life-long journey of building ecofriendly homes. Today he focuses
on cob homes, earthen structures that are built from a mix of clay, sand, and straw.
He lives in a very tiny cob house; coming in at seventy square feet it's the tiniest
home about which we interviewed the owner for this book.

Conrad told me with a chuckle that cob is "the original reclaimed material" and the
one he most likes to work with. After building and living in many types of structures including a cabin, a teepee, a yurt, and a dome house, cob seemed to be just
right for Conrad. He says, "Energetically it gives a very nice feel."

The lack of straight lines—of milled lumber with hard angles, and manufactured
surfaces—was something unique that came up in my discussion with Conrad.
While most reclaimed houses very often rely on milling and re-sawing to get the
wood into a squared shape, Conrad feels that it brought the wrong feel to homes in
which he had lived in the past.

In stark contrast to homes made with traditional milled lumber, a cob house has
curves, organic textures, and a softness. While there is wood in the space, it is
often processed in a way to keep its original form. Conrad compared this softness
to milled lumber, saying, "There is an inherent energetic violence because of the
way we harvest wood or the process it took to cut it up." It's an interesting notion—
that often the building of a home, even one that uses reclaimed materials, is inherently destructive.

Photographs by Conrad Rogue

123

This ethos permeates Conrad's approach to building with natural and reclaimed materials. This connection to the natural process of cob building is perhaps embodied by how cob is made. After combining clay, sand, and straw, cob builders often mix the substance with bare feet. It is hard not to feel a natural connection when you have cob squishing through your toes.

Photograph by Conrad Rogue

When it comes to building Conrad says, "There is always a cost to speed." With cob, there is an innate slowness to the process. "You make the decision to have a building site that is safe and pleasant." The cost of this is the time it takes to build the house, but paying that cost results in a building that "at the end of the day leaves you a stronger, healthier, and more vital person." While many people worry about how long it may take to construct such a house, Conrad suggests that misses the point. While building the home, he says, "make sure it is fun. So if it takes five years, you at least had five years of fun."

Conrad's house is comprised of an upper and lower floor. In the loft is a large sleeping space where he has his bed and storage for clothing; downstairs he segmented the space into a sitting area, a small desk, and a tiny kitchenette. The oval house—the shape gave it its name: the Jelly Bean—is only seventy square feet. It is part of a small cluster of homes that have a common house where he eats most of his meals and spends time with his fellow residents. He spends a lot of time outdoors.

Because he has the common house to fall back on, he designed his house to accommodate 70 percent of situations (sleeping, having a quite place to read a book or make a pot of tea); the remaining 30 percent are the exceptions (hosting large dinner parties, having a guest stay), and you'll adapt to accommodate them. This mentality pervades his small home: his bed will accommodate two, but there is not a guest bedroom. Since he does most of his cooking in the common house, his kitchenette is designed to make tea and a few basics things. Finally instead of having a larger entertaining space, his living-room area has seating for just a few people in a cozy setting.

The Jelly Bean initially started out as guesthouse, but as Conrad built it, he quickly became attached to it. For Conrad the small size of his home leaves him feeling safe, makes it feel cozier, and grounds him to the space. Soon after it was finished, Conrad moved into the house and since then it has become home. ⬟

ALEXIS CHRISTIAN
STEPHENS & PARSONS

TINY HOUSE ON WHEELS

- TRAVELING ACROSS THE U.S. AND CANADA
- 131 SQUARE FEET
- COMPLETED IN 2015

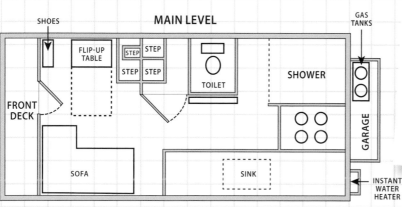

MAIN LEVEL

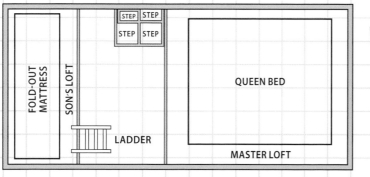

LOFT LEVEL

"I couldn't be more in love with this house. It reflects our personality like no other place I've lived."

Utilities

Electricity: 30-amp RV plug, AC power

Heating/Cooling: Electric radiator/window unit

Water: RV hookup and 20-gallon holding tank

Water Heating: Rheem Eco-sense propane tankless hot water heater

Stove: 20-inch wide Danby propane range, 4-burner; oven and broiler drawer

Refrigeration: 33-inch tall electric refrigerator

Toilet: Self-made composting toilet

Internet: ATT UnitePro Mobile Hotspot

Photograph by Christian Parsons, Tiny House Expedition

ALEXIS STEPHENS AND CHRISTIAN PARSONS ONCE TOYED WITH THE IDEA OF BUILDING a teardrop trailer, but when the thought of building a tiny house on wheels popped up, they were hooked. The pair worked with friends and family as well as a builder in Winston-Salem, NC, to bring their tiny home to life. The house was an "all-hands-on-deck" community endeavor that took eight months to complete.

Inspired by similar tiny house stories across the country, the couple was eager to get back to their filmmaking and producing roots. Christian and Alexis are the masterminds behind Tiny House Expedition, a community outreach and documentary storytelling project. For two years, they are traveling around the United States and Canada in their tiny house, documenting tiny house communities and developments. They share the stories of how tiny houses are used in eco-villages, housing for the homeless, urban infill, and everything in between. They hope the documentary will inspire discussion about sustainable and affordable housing, and encourage people to "dream big and build small."

Reclaimed materials add a lot of warmth and character to Christian and Alexis's tiny home. Inspired by 1920s bungalows and Pacific Northwest lodge-style homes, they knew they wanted to use a lot of wood and unique details in their home. A friend gave them a whole pile of raw oak boards that had been sitting unused in a tobacco barn, which they used as flooring as well as for the stairs and the porch. They got permission to dumpster dive at the local company where they bought their roof, and they found some colorful striped metal for their shower walls. Even their curtains were lovingly made from mismatched fabric remnants in shades of red and orange.

Habitat for Humanity of Forsyth County was a local sponsor that kept a lookout for secondhand materials the couple could use. The organization had been given a sixty-year-old farmhouse that was going to be demolished, and Habitat invited Christian and Alexis to take whatever they wanted. They brought friends and had a demolition party, pulling out nails and salvaging the interior and exterior wood paneling. They painted and lapped the boards to use as their wall cladding. It took a lot of time, but the character they gained for their house was worth it. As Alexis states, "I couldn't be more in love with this house because it reflects our personality like no other place I've lived."

home

Photograph by Christian Parsons, Tiny House Expedition

Christian and Alexis kept their eyes open for reclaimed materials at all times. Aside from dumpster diving, they relied on websites such as Craigslist to find odds and ends they could use. Driving by new construction sites was a great way for them to find a lot of perfectly useable plywood that otherwise would have been thrown out. Word of mouth—both in person and on social media—turned out to be a big help in finding materials. They discovered that people in the community are eager to help as long as you're not afraid to ask!

Alexis advises people interested in living small to do your research and dive in. She stresses how important it is to pare down your belongings. People may think that they can't live without all of their stuff but are later surprised by how quickly they adapt once they get rid of their clutter. "You are still you with fewer things," she says. Most of all, Christian and Alexis love the community of the tiny house movement. Their house allows them to dedicate their time and unique skills to their documentary project, which they hope will help grow the movement even more. ⬟

CHERIE SOUTHWICK

TINY HOUSE ON WHEELS
- WESTERN NORTH CAROLINA
- 169 SQUARE FEET
- COMPLETED IN 2014

MAIN LEVEL

LOFT LEVEL

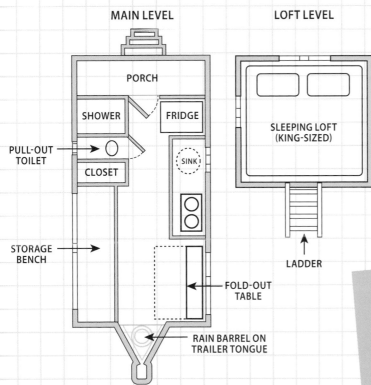

PORCH

SHOWER

FRIDGE

PULL-OUT TOILET

SINK

CLOSET

SLEEPING LOFT (KING-SIZED)

STORAGE BENCH

LADDER

FOLD-OUT TABLE

RAIN BARREL ON TRAILER TONGUE

"Anyone who is competent enough to use their hands, do a lot of research, and willing to ask for help, they'll be able to get it done."

Utilities

Electricity: Solar—four 100W panels, 12V wiring with inverter for standard appliances

Heating/Cooling: Suburban RV propane furnace (30,000 BTU)

Water: Rain water catchment for watering garden, gravity-fed kitchen sink (no plumbing)

Water Heating: Eccotemp shower instant hot water heater

Stove: Cook Mate 3100 2-burner stove (uses denatured alcohol)

Refrigeration: 12V EdgeStar refrigerator (or freezer)

Toilet: Composting toilet

Internet: Wi-Fi extender

IN HER LAST YEAR OF COLLEGE, CHERIE SOUTHWICK WAS LOOKING AHEAD TO WHAT WAS NEXT FOR HER. Knowing that she was going to have a lot of student loans and worried about finding a job, she wanted to build a tiny house so she wouldn't have to pay rent anymore. Since it was on wheels, she could take it with her if her career took her somewhere else.

She was turned on to tiny houses by her mother and sister, who were obsessed with them. At the time of writing Cherie's mother is having a tiny house built for herself and her sister is planning to build her own. Initially Cherie looked at tiny houses as an interesting concept, but it wasn't until she was facing a looming graduation date that it clicked for her.

Photograph by Laila Alamiri

Photograph by Laila Alamiri

Her building experience was limited to shop class in high school, but she had always had an interest in alternative buildings. She built her home over the course of ten months, almost entirely on her own. Now after the build, Cherie reflected back, saying, "Anyone who is competent enough to use their hands, do a lot of research, and willing to ask for help, they'll be able to get it done." While Cherie was able to figure most things out, she noted that "asking for help was the hardest part" for her.

Going into her build Cherie knew that she didn't want to have a lot of materials that would off-gas. Her studies in college all had a strong environmental focus. Both of these things led her to use reclaimed materials.

All of the lumber in her home was either reclaimed or from a sustainable lumber operation. The main framing of the house came from a program that her college, Warren Wilson, runs as part of its educational programing. Their sustainable forestry program manages land to provide lumber for local builds in a sustainable manner, focusing on selective timber cutting and ecologically minded land management.

Cherie ordered her framing materials from her school, and the rest of the materials were reclaimed. Her flooring, door, and other smaller items she found at her local ReStore. At a local construction salvage store she found all her windows, except for her skylight, which she bought new so she didn't have to worry about leaks. The insulation in her house is foam board that she found on Craigslist.

All of the curtains, cushions, and fabric elements were deconstructed dresses that Cherie purchased from Goodwill and then sewed into the final product. For her kitchen she found broken pottery and ceramic pieces and created a mosaic backsplash from them. While she loves her home she spoke at length about the amount of energy, time, and effort that goes into using reclaimed materials, saying, "People don't realize that most of your time goes into preparing for installation, not the installation itself."

All in, the house cost her $11,000 to build, including her solar panel system. Now she has a home to call her own. While she plans to stay in or near Asheville, NC, for the time being, she has options now that she has escaped the cycle of paying rent. From the outside many find the house a curiosity, but to Cherie, "it has just become normal. It has become home." ⬟

Photograph by Laila Alamiri

DAN & JESS SULLIVAN

TINY HOUSE ON WHEELS

- NORTHERN RHODE ISLAND
- 128 SQUARE FEET
- COMPLETED IN 2014

MAIN LEVEL

- BATHROOM
- KITCHEN AREA
- CLOSET SPACE
- BOOKSHELF/DESK AREA
- COUNTER-TOP/LOFT ACCESS
- STEP
- HEAT SOURCE
- DOOR
- BROOM/HAMPER CLOSET
- LOVE SEAT
- COAT-RACK/STORAGE

LOFT LEVEL

- CLOTHING STORAGE ABOVE BED
- BED
- TOP OF BOOKSHELF

"Our relationship 'is five times stronger than when we started, and it was pretty strong to begin with!'"

Utilities

Electricity: Solar

Heating/Cooling: Direct Vent propane heater

Water: Carry-in (no plumbing)

Water Heating: Stovetop

Stove: Propane RV cooktop (no oven)

Refrigeration: AC electric mini-fridge

Toilet: Composting toilet

Internet: Mobile hot spot

JESS ONCE BOUGHT A 1,500-SQUARE-FOOT TRADITIONAL HOUSE THAT SHE THOUGHT WOULD BE A QUICK REMODEL, BUT IT TURNED INTO A FIXER-UPPER THAT DEMANDED ALL HER TIME. "I was working, working on the house, or sleeping," she says. Coming from an environmentally conscious family, she started doing research on alternative housing that would be more practical. She soon met Dan and suggested the tiny house idea.

The couple decided to build their own tiny house in October 2012 and spent the winter designing it. They got started the following April and moved in during October of the next year with the interior details left to finish. Jess was traveling for work, and Dan was balancing his job and grad school, so they had to work on the tiny house during the weekends. Now married, the Sullivans are happily settled in their completed tiny house.

Jess and Dan did their best to reuse and recycle as many materials as possible in order to have an affordable, ecofriendly house. All of their windows came from Craigslist. A full-glass front door still in its packaging was another Craigslist find, worth $800 new but purchased for $125. They kept spreadsheets tallying their expenses and cost savings during the build, and they estimate that they saved more than $7,000 by using secondhand materials where they could.

They got their reclaimed insulation from a man who took apart a warehouse full of industrial coolers. All the insulation came in four-foot by eight-foot blocks, so they had to cut every piece by hand to fit them between the studs. They also had to carve grooves into the foam for all their electrical wiring. Tackling the insulation took weeks of work during one of the hottest Rhode Island summers on record.

The Sullivans used free shipping palettes for their siding. First they picked up the palettes from local manufacturing companies before other people could snatch them up for firewood. They broke the palettes apart, planed them down, cut them to the correct width, shiplapped them so they would interlock, drilled them to the exterior, and stained them all to match. It's an ongoing, time-consuming process for Dan and Jess, but it was a great way to recycle free lumber, and they love the result.

Reclaimed doors add a lot of family history to the tiny house. Two doors came from Dan's grandmother's house, and a third door came from Jess's father's house. The couple used the doors as wall partitions and loft support throughout the kitchen, bathroom, and closet areas. They even kept the windows intact, which brings light into the closet.

One of their favorite features of the house is their ceiling, made of reclaimed barn wood from 1776. A man in New Hampshire was demolishing the old barn and offered the wood for sale. Dan and Jess used the leftover barn wood to build their library shelves, desk, and pantry. They say that the richness and character of the wood can't be beat.

Photograph by Nat Rea Photography

The tiny house is a stepping stone that has allowed Dan and Jess to live their lives to the fullest. Within three months after they moved in, the house was fully paid off. They now have time to travel and do the things that are important to them. Jess has even been able to leave her corporate job and start her own business baking gluten- and dairy-free foods. And as Jess says of their relationship after building the tiny house: "It is five times stronger than when we started, and it was pretty strong to begin with!" ⬟

Photograph by Nat Rea Photography

BLAINE & MACKENZIE VOSSLER

RENOVATED 1978 AIRSTREAM

- TRAVELING ACROSS THE U.S.
- 240 SQUARE FEET
- COMPLETED IN 2014

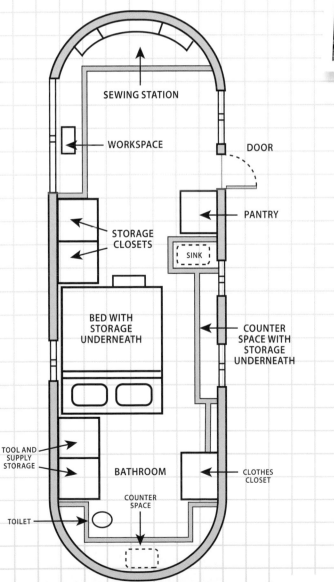

"Keep an open mind and think about different ways to use something."

Utilities

Electricity: Grid

Heating/Cooling: Electric space heaters, fans, air conditioning

Water: Water tank

Water Heating: None (propane was removed, but lines are intact)

Stove: Camp stove

Refrigeration: Mini-fridge

Toilet: Original Airstream factory model

Internet: Wi-Fi hot spot

BLAINE AND MACKENZIE VOSSLER WERE LIVING IN SAN FRANCISCO, LOOKING FOR the next step to take with their business. Together they run The Local Branch (thelocalbranch.co), making and selling clothing and leather goods with a vintage Americana vibe. With high rent prices in town and no way to open a brick-and-mortar store, the pair came up with a brilliant idea—take their business on the road with a custom Airstream!

Blaine and Mackenzie now travel full-time in their thirty-two-foot 1978 Airstream Sovereign Land Yacht, which they use as a live-in work studio. The Airstream allows them to travel to trade shows, craft fairs, and festivals all over the United States. They also run an online store, so they can sell and ship their products from anywhere in the country. Living small has eliminated their rent payment and dramatically reduced their business costs.

The couple bought the Airstream for $3,000. The bones of the trailer were good, but the interior was rough. The fridge was moldy, a window was missing, tires were flat, and there was green slime residue on the walls from cigarette smoke. They parked the trailer by the side of the road across from the ocean and got to work. It took them a couple of days to completely clean and gut the trailer. Then they hired an Airstream specialist to bring the utilities and electrical components up to snuff.

Reclaimed materials and antiques let Blaine and Mackenzie get the exact look they wanted inside their trailer. Inspired by the American West and the Airstream itself, they wanted to create a cozy cabin feeling with industrial touches. Blaine guesses they spent thirty to forty hours looking for materials and that 90 to 95 percent of everything in the trailer is reclaimed.

Photograph by The Local Branch

They found reclaimed redwood boards from a wood salvage company at a great price, and used them throughout the entire trailer to build their walls, closet, and bed. The rough-hewn wood fits their style perfectly. Mackenzie also knew exactly what kind of sink she wanted, and she found the perfect one at a high-end antique store in San Francisco. But the decimal point was in the wrong place—instead of $80, it cost $800! The next secondhand shop they visited had almost the same sink for a much better price, so they snapped it up.

Just as with the Airstream, Blaine and Mackenzie used their creativity to give old objects a new life. Old silver gutters were turned into planter boxes. Metal grain scoops found a second life as wall cubbies. The drawers under their bed are made from old fruit crates. Vintage lockers laid on their side became the base for a tabletop. Even leftover leather scraps from their business became door handles. "Keep an open mind and think about different ways to use something," Mackenzie advises. Blaine adds, "We kept the costs down by being creative."

Photograph by The Local Branch

145

As the couple discovers new storage needs, they'll pick up new antiques during their travels. Old tobacco tins and ammo boxes make great storage for pens and utensils. Even vintage breadboxes store plugs and wires. Mackenzie says that they're very choosy about which items they bring into the trailer. "It needs to be visually beautiful to us but also be really practical. You really can't have more than you need."

From start to finish, Mackenzie and Blaine had their new home in three weeks. They have adjusted quickly to their Airstream lifestyle. "The hardest things about living on the road aren't so hard because we're always waking up in a cool new place, and seeing parts of the country we've never been to before," Mackenzie says. ⬟

Photograph by The Local Branch

CLOSING

The tiny homes featured in this book are unique, much like their owners. The use of reclaimed materials in tiny houses allow for beautiful homes to be built that are both budget-friendly and do their part for the environment. The combination of diverting materials from the waste stream and the small size of the house all contribute to a lighter footprint when it comes to where we live.

Tiny houses have captured the imagination and attention of many, primarily because of their design. Each house is different, and the use of reclaimed materials adds to this profoundly. The stories, the history, and beauty coming from old barn wood and fixtures of years gone by all add to the next chapter in these homes.

RESOURCES

Interviewee Websites

http://aaronmaret.com

http://aatinyhouse.wordpress.com

http://dominiquemoody.com

http://forvillagers.com

www.housealive.org

http://thelocalbranch.co

http://tinyhallhouse.tumblr.com

www.facebook.com/ourtinyhouseview.barringtontinyhouse

www.hummingbirdmicrohomes.com

www.katefoxmicroholding.co.uk

www.livinginatinyhouse.blogspot.com

www.rhizhome.com

www.tinycommunitycenter.com

www.tinyhouseexpedition.com

www.rockymountaintinyhouses.com

www.theupcyclist.com.au

http://thelittlecabinunderthebigtreehousenearthesmallriver.yolasite.com

General Tiny House Websites

TheTinyLife.com

TinyHouseBlog.com

TinyHouseMagazine.co

MiniMotives.com

TinyHouseTalk.com

Tiny-Project.com

TinyHouseListings.com

TinyHouseSwoon.com

RowdyKittens.com

TinyHouseBuild.com

PADTinyHouses.com

Relaxshacks.blogspot.com

TinyHouseGiantJourney.com

NicheDesignBuild.com

ThisIsTheLittleLife.com

SolHausDesign.com

ABedOverMyHead.com

BoneyardStudios.org

ChrisAndMalissa.com

TheTinyHouse.net

120SquareFeet.com

TinyHouseOnThePrairie.net

TinyHouseTeacher.com

LittleYellowDoor.wordpress.com

Shelterwise.com

TinyrEvolution.us

Tiny House Books

Diedricksen, Derek. *Humble Homes, Simple Shacks, Cozy Cottages, Ramshackle Retreats, Funky Forts: And Whatever the Heck Else We Could Squeeze in Here* (Guilford, CT: Lyons Press, 2012).

Diedricksen, Derek. *Microshelters* (North Adams, MA: Storey Publishing, 2015).

Kahn, Lloyd. *Tiny Homes: Simple Shelter* (Bolinas, CA: Shelter Publications, 2012).

Mitchell, Ryan. *Cracking the Code: A Guide to Building Codes & Zoning for Tiny Houses* (Asheville, NC: Ryan Mitchell, 2013).

Mitchell, Ryan. *The New Retirement* (Asheville, NC: Ryan Mitchell, n.d.).

Mitchell, Ryan. *Shockingly Simple Electrical for Tiny Houses* (Asheville, NC: Ryan Mitchell, n.d.).

Mitchell, Ryan. *Tiny House Living* (Cincinnati, OH: Betterway Home Books, 2014).

Rowan, Gerald. *Compact Cabins* (North Adams, MA: Storey Publishing, 2010).

Williams, Dee. *The Big Tiny* (New York: Blue Rider Press, 2014).

INDEX

Note: Page numbers in **bold** indicate tiny house owner stories/ examples, and page numbers in *italics* indicate floor plans.

A

Airstreams, as tiny houses
  Stacy's Airstream (California), **49–54**
  Vossler, Blaine and Mackenzie (traveling U.S.), **141–46**
Anson, April (Oregon), **37–42**
Appliances, large. *See specific appliances*
Apps, for reclaimed materials, 22–23

B

Barn wood
  ceiling example, 139
  finding/procuring, 34
  flooring example, 53, 54
  quality of, 34
  reclaiming, 34
  siding example, 92
Barrington family (Colorado), **43–48**

Books, on tiny houses, 151

C

Cavanagh, Makayla (Washington), **55–60**
Cob house, **121–26**
Cooktops. *See* Stove options, examples
Cost of tiny houses, 10–11. *See also* Owner experiences
Craigslist, for materials/ sources
  about, 22, 27, 34
  examples, 46, 47, 58, 77, 81, 136, 138

D

Design of tiny houses, 11–12

E

Electricity options, example
  AC/DC. *See also* solar/ battery
Electricity options, examples
  AC/DC, *89*
  grid/hookup options, *37, 43, 49, 55, 71, 79, 83, 89, 97, 111, 115, 127, 141*

multiple options, *49, 79, 89*
  solar/battery, *37, 49, 61, 67, 79, 101, 105, 121, 133, 137*
Estimating material requirements, 19–22

F

Flooring
  barn wood example, 53, 54
  owner's stories, 41, 46, 58, 81, 98, 114, 130, 136
  reclaiming, 33–34
Foundation, tiny houses on
  Miller, Mark (Wisconsin), **97–100**
  Rogue, Conrad (Oregon), **121–26**
Fox, Kate, and Andy Gill (United Kingdom), **61–66**
Freecycle, 23
Furnace types. *See* Heating/cooling options, examples

G

Galletly, James (Australia), **67–70**

Gill, Andy, and Kate Fox (United Kingdom), **61–66**

H

Hall family (Massachusetts), **71–78**
Hastings, Sarah (Massachusetts), **79–82**
Heating/cooling options, examples
  Airstream unit, *49, 141*
  ceiling fan, *55, 71, 79, 97*
  electric baseboard heat, *97*
  electric heaters, *37, 115, 127. See also* portable/space heater
  Envi heater, *55, 71*
  fans, *101, 115*
  LG mini split, *43*
  none, *67*
  olive oil candles and tiny can stove, *121*
  portable/space heater, *83, 101, 111, 141*
  propane heater/ furnace, *89, 105, 133, 137*

Heating/cooling
options, examples
—*continued*
window air
conditioner, *127*
wood-burning
fireplace, *97*
wood-burning stove,
61, 79, 105

J

Jointers and planers,
29–30

K

Kesler, Zee (British
Columbia), **83–88**

M

Maret, Aaron (traveling
U.S.), **89–96**
Miller, Mark
(Wisconsin), **97–100**
Milling lumber, 27
Moody, Dominique
(California),
101–4

N

Nails
in pallets, 33
removing screws and,
28–29, 33
tools for removing,
26, 29
Networking, for
materials, 23

O

Owner (interviewee)
websites, 149
Owner experiences

adjusting to tiny
house, 38–39, 48,
51–52, 96
appeal of reclaimed/
sustainable
materials, 64, 75,
91, 93–95, 103,
109, 128, 145
building tiny houses,
56–57, 63–64, 69,
72, 85–86, 88,
102, 107, 112–14,
135
buying new things,
60, 77, 95
cob house, 122–26
cost to build, 60, 88,
92, 125, 136
design approaches,
41, 53–54, 63,
69–70, 75, 80–81,
84–85, 86, 103–4,
110, 114, 116, 119,
123, 125–27, 130,
136, 143–45
flooring, 41, 46, 58,
81, 98, 114, 130,
136
gathering reclaimed
materials, 39–42,
45–47, 54, 58–59,
64, 69–70, 75–77,
80–81, 86–87, 92,
98, 99–100, 103–4,
107, 114, 118–19,
120, 130–32, 136,
138–39
moving the house,
65–66
paring down
belongings/clutter,
78, 132

processing reclaimed
materials, 47, 108
reasons for going
tiny, 38, 44, 50, 56,
62–63, 68, 72, 75,
80, 84, 90–91, 98,
102, 106, 112, 128,
134, 138, 142
storage solutions,
59, 81, 87, 114,
143–45, 146. *See
also specific floor
plan diagrams*
storied reclaimed
wood, 103
storing materials, 86,
92, 99, 100
winning over
skeptics, 52–53

P

Pallets
breaking down, 33
chemical-treatment
warning, 33
finding/procuring, 32
intact, using in
structure, 33
reclaiming, 33–34
wood quality, 32
Parham, Greg
(Colorado), **105–10**
Parsons, Christian,
and Alexis Stephens
(traveling U.S./
Canada), **127–32**
Planers, 27, 29–31
Pollard, Natalie (North
Carolina), **111–14**
Processing reclaimed
wood, 26–31
about: overview of, 26

creating uniformity,
30–31
deconstruction
process, 27–30
de-nailing process,
28–29
identifying desirable
pieces, 28
milling/re-sawing
lumber, 27
resurfacing process,
29–30
safety equipment for,
27–28
tools for, 26–27

R

Reclaimed materials.
See also Wood,
reclaimed
about: major
considerations for
reclaiming, 19
appeal of, 10
apps for, 22–23
assessing
possibilities, 23–24
benefits of, 12
budget-friendliness
of, 14
challenge with, 19
defined, 13
ecofriendly nature of,
14–15
estimating
requirements,
19–22
evaluating, 24–26
importance for
future, 17–18
networking for, 23
quality of, 15

reasons for using, 13–18

recycled and, 13

role in tiny houses, 10

sourcing. *See* Sourcing reclaimed materials

storing, 32

types of materials, 13

uniquenesses of, 15–17

Reclaiming materials, 19–34

Refrigerator options, examples

cool box on north wall, *121*

electric, *43, 71, 111, 115, 127. See also* mini-fridge

electric/propane, *49, 89*

lidded crate under hut, *61*

mini-fridge, *55, 79, 97, 105, 137, 141*

none, *67, 83*

standard, *37*

3-way (propane, AC, DC), *89*

12-volt, *101, 133*

Resources

books, 151

general websites, 150

interviewee websites, 149

Resurfacing wood, 29–30

Roberts, Gareth (British Columbia), **115–20**

Rogue, Conrad (Oregon), **121–26**

S

Safety equipment, 27–28

Sanders, 27, 30

Sanding wood, 30

Saws, 27

Sizes of tiny houses, examples

about: range of sizes, 9

less than 100 square feet, **61–66**, **67–70**, **121–26**

100-149 square feet, **37–42**, **55–60**, **101–4**, **127–32**, **137–40**

150-199 square feet, **71–78**, **79–82**, **83–88**, **89–96**, **105–10**, **115–20**, **133–36**

200-249 square feet, **43–48**, **49–54**, **97–100**, **141–46**

250+ square feet, **111–14**

Sourcing reclaimed materials

apps for, 22–23

assessing sources/ materials, 23–24

from barn wood, 34

common source materials, 32–34

evaluating materials, 24–26

from flooring, 33–34

networking for, 23

from pallets, 32–33

places to find materials, 22–24

storing and, 32

Southwick, Cherie (North Carolina), **133–36**

Stacy's Airstream (California), **49–54**

Stephens, Alexis, and Christian Parsons (traveling U.S./ Canada), **127–32**

Storing reclaimed wood, 32

Stove options, examples

camp stove, *141*

convection, *71*

cooktop, *89, 101, 115, 137*

denatured alcohol, *133*

hot plate, *79*

induction cooktop (portable), *101*

microwave, *43, 79, 97*

none, *67, 83*

propane, *127, 137*

propane/gas, *37, 43, 49, 55, 89, 105, 111*

single-burner, 71, 121

toaster oven, *79*

wood-burning, *61*

Sullivan, Dan and Jess (Rhode Island), **137–40**

T

Table saws, 27

Tiny House Expedition, about, 128

Tiny houses

appeal of, 9, 11–12

attention to detail, 12

cost of, 10–11

design of, 11–12

principles defining, 9

size range, 9

Tiny houses, examples of

about: overview/ summary of, 36, 147

by size. *See* Sizes of tiny houses, examples

by utility or appliance type. *See specific utility or appliance*

on foundations. *See* Foundation, tiny houses on

on wheels. *See* Airstreams, as tiny houses; Wheels, tiny houses on

Toilet options, examples

Airstream original model, *141*

composting, *55, 71, 105, 111, 115, 133, 137*

composting (custom), *79, 89, 127*

marine biodegradable, *101*

none, *61, 67, 83, 121*

outdoor, *97*

RV, *37, 43, 49*

Tools, for processing wood, 26–27

U

Uniformity of materials, 30–31

Utilities, types of. *See specific utilities*

V

Vossler, Blaine and Mackenzie (traveling U.S.), *141–46*

W

Walls
  materials requirements, 20, 21–22. *See also* Processing reclaimed wood; Wood, reclaimed
  uniformity of boards for, 30–31
Water heating options, examples
  electric and propane, *49–54*
  microwave, *97–100*
  none, *67–70*, *83–88*, *89–96*, *121–26*, *141–46*
  propane, *49–54*, *115–20*. *See also* tankless/on-demand
  reduction cooktop, thermos storage, *101–4*
  stovetop, *137–40*
  tankless/on-demand, *37–42*, *43–48*, *55–60*, *71–78*, *79–82*, *105–10*, *111–14*, *127–32*, *133–36*
  wood-burning stove, *61–66*
Water source options, examples

carried in, *111–14*, *137–40*
grid, *37–42*, *115–20*
grid/off-grid, *49–54*
hose hookup/tank, *55–60*, *71–78*, *79–82*, *83–88*, *89–96*, *105–10*, *127–32*, *141–46*
Jerry can and pump, *61–66*
none, *67–70*
rain water, *121–26*, *133–36*
various containers, *61–66*, *101–4*, *121–26*
water cooler, *97–100*
well, *43–48*
Websites. *See* Resources
Wheels, tiny houses on. *See also* Airstreams, as tiny houses
Anson, April (Oregon), *37–42*
Barrington family (Colorado), *43–48*
Cavanagh, Makayla (Washington), *55–60*
Fox, Kate, and Andy Gill (United Kingdom), *61–66*
Galletly, James (Australia), *67–70*
Hall family (Massachusetts), *71–78*
Hastings, Sarah (Massachusetts), *79–82*

Kesler, Zee (British Columbia), *83–88*
Maret, Aaron (traveling U.S.), *89–96*
Moody, Dominique (California), *101–4*
Parham, Greg (Colorado), *105–10*
Pollard, Natalie (North Carolina), *111–14*
Roberts, Gareth (British Columbia), *115–20*
Southwick, Cherie (North Carolina), *133–36*
Stephens, Alexis, and Christian Parsons (traveling U.S./Canada), *127–32*
Sullivan, Dan and Jess (Rhode Island), *137–40*
Wood, reclaimed. *See also* Processing reclaimed wood
  assessing possibilities, 23–24
  availability and milling procedures, 12–13
  budget-friendliness of, 14
  character of, 15–16
  defined, 13
  dimensions of, 16–17
  ecofriendly nature of, 14–15

  estimating requirements, 19–22
  evaluating, 24–26
  importance for future, 17–18
  industrial product waste, 13
  networking for, 23
  pallets, 13, 26, 30, 32–33
  pros and cons summary, 17
  quality of materials, 15
  reasons for using, 13–18
  recaptured products, 13
  recycling processes, 13
  sourcing. *See* Sourcing reclaimed materials
  stories associated with, 17
  uniquenesses of, 15–17
  wall requirements, 20, 21–22

ABOUT THE AUTHOR

Ryan Mitchell lives in Charlotte, North Carolina, and has been active in the tiny house movement for years. You might know him as the main blogger and founder of TheTinyLife.com, a website dedicated to sharing stories of tiny living—whether it's tips for simplifying your life or advice for building your own tiny residence. Because nothing beats one-on-one interactions, Ryan helps people connect with each other through community events at TinyHouseConference.com.

Since Ryan built his own tiny house in 2013, he has been able to actively pursue his passions, which include photography, backpacking, and travel. Ryan believes that alternative housing options and sustainable local agriculture are key components to meet the future needs of society.